BATTLEWORN

THE MEMOIR OF A COMBAT MEDIC IN AFGHANISTAN

CHANTELLE TAYLOR

BATTLEWORN
THE MEMOIR OF A COMBAT MEDIC IN AFGHANISTAN

iUniverse Star
an iUniverse imprint

iUniverse books may be ordered through booksellers or by contacting:

iUniverse
1663 Liberty Drive
Bloomington, IN 47403
www.iuniverse.com
1-800-Authors (1-800-288-4677)

Because of the dynamic nature of the Internet, any web addresses or
links contained in this book may have changed since publication and
may no longer be valid. The views expressed in this work are solely those
of the author and do not necessarily reflect the views of the publisher,
and the publisher hereby disclaims any responsibility for them.

ISBN: 978-1-5320-0385-1 (sc)
ISBN: 978-1-5320-0851-1 (hc)
ISBN: 978-1-5320-0386-8 (e)

Library of Congress Control Number: 2014902837

Print information available on the last page.

iUniverse rev. date: 10/12/2016

For my brother David
(1970–2002)

CONTENTS

PREFACE

The following account is based on my experience as the lead trauma medic within an infantry fighting company. I have endeavoured to report events accurately and truthfully; insult or injury to any of the parties described or quoted herein, or to their families, is unintentional.

After putting my thoughts on paper over a period of six weeks in the late summer of 2009, I decided to send the raw text to my mum, trying to explain what I had experienced in Afghanistan as a serving soldier. It wasn't polished, and it only touched the surface of my time with B Company 5 Scots (5th Battalion, the Royal Regiment of Scotland) during their mission to hold Nad-e Ali. She wrote back, commenting that my writing was developing into a good story and that she enjoyed reading about the characters, particularly young Duffy.

I would never have contemplated writing this book if it hadn't been for Mum's encouragement. I have enjoyed a lifetime of her wisdom: 'You can stoop down and pick up anything, Channy; try reaching for it instead.'

In *Battleworn*, I tell the story of B Company, a beleaguered group of individuals who fought relentlessly and against all odds to hold Nad-e Ali, a Taliban stronghold in southern Afghanistan, in 2008.

It is difficult for soldiers to express feelings whilst engaged in combat, as training rightly teaches suppression of emotion in order to survive the battlefield. I wrote the following poem for Cpl Stu Pearson QGM (3 PARA) and Cpl Mark Wright GC (3 PARA). I share it here in honour of all our fallen.

Keep Me Awake – Kajaki

Lying still, like the Tommy did before me,
My trench is in a land far from her heart;
A purple horizon has become my solace, my
peace.

Don't fall asleep, soldier, for you may not wake
again.

Body broken, I still breathe.
Who is that, who lies beside me?
I am your brother; you are my keeper.

Don't fall asleep, soldier, for you may not wake
again.

What is your name?
I am a fallen soldier; keep me awake, let me see
her face once more.
I will, I will ...

Don't fall asleep, soldier, for you will not wake
again.

LIST OF **ABBREVIATIONS** AND **ACRONYMS**

2IC: second in command

2Lt: second lieutenant

2 PARA/3 PARA: 2nd/3rd Battalion, the Parachute Regiment

ABTF: Airborne Task Force

ANA: Afghan National ANP: Afghan National Police

AO: area of operations

ASM: air to surface missile

ATV: all-terrain vehicle

Brig.: brigadier

CAP: company aid post

Capt.: captain

CAS: close air support

casevac: casualty evacuation

cat-A: category A (wound classification)

cat-B: category B (wound classification)

cat-C: category C (wound classification)

CCP: casualty collection point

CLP: combat logistic patrol

CMT: combat medical technician

CP: command post

Cpl: corporal

CSAR: combat search and rescue

CSgt: colour sergeant

DEFAC: dining facility

DOS: Department of State

evac: evacuation

FCO: Foreign and Commonwealth Office

FOB: forward operating base

FSG: fire support group

Fus: fusilier

GC: George Cross

GM: George Medal

GPMG: general purpose machine gun

HE: high explosive

HLZ: helicopter landing zone

HQ: headquarters

ICOM: interim communications operations method

ID: intradermal

IDF: indirect fire

IED: improvised explosive device

IM: intramuscular

intel: intelligence

ITC: infantry training centre

IV: intravenous

JTAC: joint tactical air controller

KAF: Kandahar Air Force Base

KAIA: Kabul International Airport

KIA: killed in action

LCpl: lance corporal

LKG: Lashkar Gah

LOCSTAT: location with grid reference

Lt: lieutenant

Lt Col: lieutenant colonel

Maj.: major

MARCH-P: acronym for emergency medical assessment (*see* text for details)

MERT: medical emergency response team

MOB: main operating base

MOD: Ministry of Defence

MREs: meals ready to eat

NHS: National Health Service

NVG: night vision goggles

OC: officer commanding

OMLT: operational mentor and liaison team

ops: operations

PB: patrol base

PEF: poppy eradication force

PF: Pathfinder

PK/PKM: Polemyot Kalashnikov machine gun

PMT: police mentoring team

POW: prisoner of war

PRT: provincial reconstruction team

PSD: personal security detail

Pte: private

PTSD: post-traumatic stress disorder

PX: post exchange

QGM: Queen's Gallantry Medal

QRF: quick reaction force

RAF: Royal Air Force

RAP: regimental aid post

recce: reconnaissance

reorg: reorganisation

resupp: resupply

RI: Royal Irish

RIP: relief in place

RLC: Royal Logistics Corp

RPG: rocket propelled grenade

RRF: Royal Regiment of Fusiliers

SAM: surface to air missile

SC: subcutaneous

Sgt: sergeant

Sgt Maj.: sergeant major

sitrep: situation report

SME: subject matter expert

SNCO: senior non-commissioned officer

SUSAT: sight unit small arms trilux

TA: territorial army

TAB: tactical advance to battle

UAV: unmanned aerial vehicle

VP: vulnerable point

WMIK: weapons mounted installation kit

THE MAN IN THE ARENA

It is not the critic who counts; not the man who points out how the strong man stumbles, or where the doer of deeds could have done them better. The credit belongs to the man who is actually in the arena, whose face is marred by dust and sweat and blood; who strives valiantly; who errs, who comes short again and again, because there is no effort without error and shortcoming; but who does actually strive to do the deeds; who knows great enthusiasms, the great devotions; who spends himself in a worthy cause; who at the best knows in the end the triumph of high achievement, and who at the worst, if he fails, at least fails while daring greatly, so that his place shall never be with those cold and timid souls who neither know victory nor defeat.

—*Theodore Roosevelt*

[AUTHOR'S NOTE: 'The Man in the Arena' is an excerpt from Theodore Roosevelt's *Citizenship in a Republic* speech given at the Sorbonne in Paris, France, on 23 April 1910. These are the words carried by my grandfather whilst serving in Korea in 1951 as a 41 Commando Royal Marine.]

PROLOGUE

The first explosion rocked the vehicle, smashing my head against the front of the wagon. I could hear rounds zipping through the antennas above me. 'What the fuck?' I shouted as an array of munitions continued to rain down on us.

I was in the same vehicle as LCpl Kevin Coyle, the signaller of the officer commanding (OC). The lightly armoured patrol in which I was travelling had turned into a Taliban shooting gallery; the noise from left and rear incoming fire was deafening. Our heavy machine guns roared into action as broken bricks and clouds of dust enveloped us.

Our Land Rover, the second vehicle in the packet, was taking sustained and heavy fire. Looking up through the hatch, I could see rounds pinging from left to right. I guessed they were from enemy fighters on my side of the vehicle. I heard someone shout, 'Get some fucking rounds down!'

Popping back up through the hatch for a split second, I got eyes on an insurgent who was engaging us, thirty metres away and to the half right of me. Suddenly overwhelmed by the fear that I was about to be shot in the face, I experienced a rush of blood to the head and took in a mouthful of dust. Reminding myself to breathe, I engaged him instinctively and purposefully. I didn't stop firing until he dropped.

The excitement that I felt before moving into Marjah had faded fast. Kev, covering our right side, engaged another fighter close by. The machine gunner in the vehicle behind us took on two insurgents who had positioned themselves on the roof of a compound.

Shouting out half of a fire control order, I alerted my team to other targets around us. A lull in the firefight commenced just then, soon followed by the dreaded cry 'man down, man down!' blasting across the radio net.

As I scanned for further threats, Maj. Harry Clark, our OC, shouted through to the back of our Land Rover, 'Man down in the rear vehicle!'

He calmly jumped out of the front seat as I climbed through the back door to meet him. We started to run to the back of the patrol, stopping to take cover along the way, both of us vulnerable to enemy fire all the while. Fighting the unforgiving Afghan sun, we made light work of the distance we covered on foot. My medical pack felt like a lead weight on my back.

Midway there, the OC stopped and turned back towards our vehicle. Unconcerned, I followed him. It wasn't through lack of interest that I said nothing; my lungs simply needed oxygen far more than I needed conversation. I jumped back into the wagon and struggled to breathe.

Kev laughed. 'You okay, Channy?'

I wanted to share the joke that I was in and out of our vehicle like a yo-yo, but I was 'hanging out' – physically exhausted.

Shunting forward, the wagon hastily moved off. Back on top cover, covering my arcs again, I was desperate to cool down. I gulped water quickly, trying to avoid becoming nauseated. The heat radiating around my cumbersome and oversized helmet finally started to ease off. Slowly I regained my composure. Kev continued to laugh at my struggling to run in the midday heat.

Our minor break in contact allowed us time to get out of the initial kill zone, and we managed to limp to an area of open space: it was large enough to land a Chinook, making it the perfect choice for a casualty extraction.

The OC sent two of our company snipers up onto a compound roof. They gave us over watch as we prepared an all-round defence. As the men of B Company covered the outer cordon, our snipers' body count began to rise. The Apache gunship was now on station; visually scanning the ground from the sky, the crew hunted the Taliban of Marjah.

Chuckie had taken a round to the abdomen; he was manning the .50-calibre machine gun in the rear vehicle. His Land Rover had screeched past our own when the OC shouted for our call sign to go firm in the open space. Chuckie was lying in the back of his vehicle with Commander Cpl Greg Gorman; Greg had administered the initial treatment which had earlier saved me from running a further half kilometre to the back of our patrol. Our OC's decision to stop midway and turn back had prevented us both from becoming casualties. There's a fine line between bravery and stupidity.

'Channy, he's been hit in the gut, I cannae see where it's come out.' Greg's familiar Scottish accent carried a worried tone, and sweat dripped from his anxious-looking face.

When I eventually got hands on Chuckie, we were still in contact with enemy fire, so I had to assess his wounds quickly: I had about thirty seconds to surmise what was happening inside of him. His wound was fairly high up so I was inclined to think that he might have sustained a chest injury, which meant that his evacuation needed to be swift. Wounds to the abdomen are problematic at best of times, add to that a chest injury, and Chuckie's day would end badly. His chances of survival were slim if we could not get him back to more-definitive care. Bleeding in the abdominal cavity is almost impossible to control, so we positioned him as best we could with the equipment that we had. We sat him up with his knees pulled against his chest, which would at least form some type of compression without restricting his breathing too much. Leaving further treatment to company medic Tom Rooke ('Rookey'), I made my way back to brief the OC on our casualty's condition.

Casualty extraction under fire wasn't without risk either; the inbound Chinook was escorted by two Apache gunships, which circled our position like birds of prey before the lone bird swept in. Airborne within thirty minutes of being hit, our team had gotten lucky. Reassured, I sorted my kit out before mounting up with Kev, Greg, and the rest of B Company. This was my first taste of close-quarter combat; little did I know that B Company would be under fire almost every day for the next two months.

CHAPTER 1

GAME ON

WELL ON OUR WAY INTO OUR TOUR OF HELMAND PROVINCE, B Company receives orders to patrol into Nad-e Ali, just north of the main British operating base of Lashkar Gah.

Our convoy moves cautiously across the desert. We hear the thud of several explosions ahead, the noise carried on the dry air. As vehicles chunter along, every soldier nurses the uneasy thought as to what may lie ahead.

After leaving our base, we head north-west. In total we are a force of just sixty-two troops drawn from two platoons, travelling in ten heavily armed vehicles. Many of our soldiers are very young. We range in age from eighteen to late thirties, with the average age at around twenty-two. This is the first tour of Afghanistan for some. At thirty-two, it's my second tour and would become my last as a serving British soldier. In this unbearable heat we are laden in heavy uncomfortable body armour and helmets, scanning the desert for anything that could pose a threat. Our company will carry out what is known as a 'look see' patrol to Nad-e Ali, just fifteen kilometres north-west of Lashkar Gah (capital of Helmand Province).

Our mission has come about as a direct result of a sharp

increase in enemy activity. There has been speculation that a company from one of the parachute battalions would be committed to this area, but many are now assigned to a major operation which the brigade has been planning for some time, consuming much of its manpower.

It involves the delivery of a three-hundred-ton turbine by convoy from Kandahar across open desert to the hydroelectric dam at Kajaki. The dam was built in 1975 with funding from US Aid, an American development charity, but only two turbines were supplied before the Soviets invaded Afghanistan in 1979. Work then stalled, and the dam was unable to fully function. In 2006, when British troops arrived, one of the first projects identified to help the local populace was to complete the work at the dam.

In 2008, 16 Brigade took on this responsibility as a 'main effort', a huge undertaking requiring the majority of our assets. The mission was to complete the move of a third turbine and additional mechanical items to the dam. It was hoped that the task would allow contractors to commission the system and generate electricity for the entirety of Helmand Province.

Insurgents gathering in Nad-e Ali presented an unwelcome distraction: if they disrupted the convoy and forced the brigade commander to detach manpower from the Kajaki task, there was a risk that the operation as a whole would be compromised. Any commander wishing to progress recognises early that he must win the propaganda war, and getting the turbine in place would be a major coup. Success would mean 'lighting up' Helmand and therefore, a sizable boost for the hearts-and-minds campaign.

I lead a team of three medics, and I feel responsible for the young Jocks that we support. (Jock is the nickname given to the private soldiers of any Scottish infantry battalion.) I am also always mindful that every journey we make over the bomb-infested highways of Helmand might be the last for someone. Our job is to patrol in and around the area and report back on the mood of the town and its people. If you find children playing outside their homes and people in the markets, then 'atmospherics' are judged as good. If the streets are deserted and the locals are non-existent, then this paints a picture of uncertainty – an attack of some kind is often imminent.

The lead vehicles create a sand screen, which cuts our visibility to almost zero. I'm on top cover, along with Kev Coyle, our signaller. Our position gives the driver and commander a 360-degree visual scan of the ground we're passing over and the road ahead, letting them gauge potential threats. We man the open turret on top of the vehicle; our interpreter sits quietly in the back, asleep if he has any sense. If there's an insurgent out there looking to take us on, the top cover usually gets hit first. I can taste the grit in my mouth from the dirt and dust kicked up ahead of us.

Kev, B Company's signaller, has an Italian look about him – jet-black hair, olive skin, and blue eyes – and his dry sense of humour is an acquired taste. I have finally warmed to it through the hours we spend together on the ground.

'This is fucking shit!' Kev grunts.

'It doesn't look like we are stopping any time soon, either,' I reply.

'Eight more weeks, and that's us.'

Our conversation is interrupted by an explosion, closer than the others were. A spiral of smoke rises into the air in the middle distance. My first thought is that it is a drop short mortar round, but it appears that we aren't the intended target. The explosion is closer to the town centre than it is to us.

Kev turns to me with a grin. 'Game on, mucker,' he shouts, barely audible over the noise of the engine. I read his lips in order to make out what he's just said as we hit what seems like every pothole on this track. Kev and I have been battle buddies for a fair time, patrolling the district centres of Lash and Nawa, more recently involved in a gnarly ambush in the notorious area of Marjah.

Our convoy consists of ten lightly armoured Land Rovers, consisting of the snatch version and the open-top weapons mounted installation kit (WMIK). The WMIK is a stripped-down Land Rover that comes with a series of roll bars and special weapons mounts. It was designed primarily as a reconnaissance (recce for short) and fire support vehicle. The rear roll bar cage features a well in which a gunner can stand and swing his weapon in a 360-degree arc of fire from a rail-mounted system.

The rear station can be fitted with a .50-calibre heavy machine gun, a 40 mm grenade launcher, or a 7.62 mm general purpose machine gun (GPMG). American troops thought that we were crazy to drive about in open-top vehicles, until I explained that our guys survived improvised explosive device (IED) attacks because they were blown out of the vehicle as opposed to getting thrown against the heavy armour inside.

That much is true; however, the variant that's housing Kev and me is not so clever. It's the 'snatch' Land Rover. It was designed for tasks in Northern Ireland and deployed disastrously to Basra, in southern Iraq, after the initial invasion. It was later shipped to Helmand, and it became the focus of media controversy after numerous incidents which resulted in fatalities in both Iraq and Afghanistan.

It was nothing more than a money-saving choice for Helmand, and I was unlucky enough to become very familiar with the machine (and grateful not to be the interpreter sitting in the back). Its box body was not fit for the purpose: anyone sitting in the rear would often boil, even with the later addition of air conditioning. Limited armour also ensured that it would not withstand small arms for prolonged periods, let alone any type of high-energy explosive.

Spending hours in any vehicle will give you an intimate look at all the good and bad points, and this knowledge is priceless to those buying such equipment. Trialling a military kit could be done far more effectively if the terrain on which it is trialled is similar to the place where it ends up operationally. Testing the snatch Land Rover in Lashkar Gah is a lot like throwing a child into the deep end of a swimming pool and expecting him to immediately start swimming like Michael Phelps.

Lash is where the provincial reconstruction team (PRT) is based. They are a joint team comprised of Foreign and Commonwealth Office (FCO) staff and civilian advisors from the Ministry of Defence (MOD). With military support, they plan the strategic development and reconstruction of the region. Based on this information, I figured we'd be out of the base for forty-eight hours maximum, and I packed my kit and equipment accordingly.

Meanwhile, our vehicles continue to progress through the desert, the drivers peering through the thick sandstorm our convoy has whipped up. I breathe in diesel fumes mixed with the dry, musky scent of the desert. The smell of diesel and hot air instantly reminds me of time spent in Iraq in the summer of 2003. In the stifling heat, I am thirsty and my back is soaking wet. My skull bakes like pie crust inside my helmet.

Afghanistan is landlocked in the bowl of the Hindu Kush, with mountains that go on forever. The landscape is severe but beautiful, and the place has a biblical feel to it. I served in Iraq, Kosovo, and Sierra Leone, but nowhere else is like Afghanistan – it isn't just another country … it's another mindset.

Winters are bleak, and summers are marked by cloudless

blue skies, with temperatures topping 140 degrees. The dry climate and harsh environment have the ability to deliver beauty in the springtime as the fields of Helmand blossom with red-pink flowers. The 'death crop' of southern Afghanistan is harvested from these fields. While in full flower, the opium poppies present a picture-perfect look, but for many years they have funded war and criminality.

More than 90 per cent of the world's heroin supply comes from poppies cultivated here. The country's illegal drug business generates $4 billion a year – half the nation's gross domestic product.[1] A big slice of this money buys the Taliban the guns that we are driving towards.

These facts flit through my brain as we drive along. We often hear in briefings that thirty Taliban have been killed here, another forty there. But they just keep coming, in their kameezes and worn-out shoes. The kameez is part of the traditional way of dress for local Afghan men, its light fabric making it the perfect choice for the harsh sun of Afghanistan. It has an adopted layer system; you can add layers or take them away as you wish. In the extreme cold, Afghans use a blanket as a type of shawl; their traditional dress suits the environment perfectly. Observing their attire has caused me to wonder why we haven't adopted a policy of using examples of the local attire during wartime, and making it work for us. We disadvantage ourselves by not thinking like the indigenous population; to succeed you must know your enemy. We have the firepower, but what they have is time. We drive them out of different districts; they flee to the mountains, and wait. We pacify a town, maybe reopen a school. When we leave, they come back and tear the building down

---

1   UNODC, *World Drug Report 2012*, www.unodc.org/unodc/en/data-andanalysis/WDR-2012.html, last accessed 1 October 2013.

again. They are like the hydra, the Greek mythical creature that had the ability to grow new heads. You kill a Taliban fighter, and his eight brothers all become recruits for jihad. We're fighting terror; they're doped up on a holy war.

My thoughts keep drifting along these lines, and I am aware that none of it is likely to ever change. The vehicle jolts, ending my reverie. Our convoy has come to a halt on the outskirts of Nad-e Ali. The two platoon sergeants, Monty Monteith and Scotty McFadden, get out of their vehicles and walk among the tired and bored troops to ensure that all is as it should be. Monty and Scotty are old friends. Monty's weathered appearance is a look reserved for the hardened soldiers of the infantry. Scotty seems to have fared far better in avoiding the harsh 'ten years older' weather of the Brecon Beacons beating on his face. (Brecon, Wales, houses the military's Infantry Training Centre [ITC].)

Right now the boss, Maj. Harry Clark, relaxes, secure in the knowledge that both Monty and Scotty are squaring things away on his behalf. With some vehicle engines switched off, I can hear a little better, and I listen to the sound of explosions across town. More black smoke rises, and the distinctive rattle of sporadic small-arms fire sounds. It's no big deal, and everyone on this patrol has seen and heard it all before.

I climb down from top cover and sit in a pool of my own sweat, feeling tired from the long day.

Kev looks down at me. 'We should get some scoff on,' he says in an agitated voice.

I hadn't realised until then that I was starving. When you're tired, your blood-sugar count gets low, and your stomach starts to rumble. I am carrying biscuits brown and pâté, a light meal from my ration pack, and it smells like cat food. It probably tastes the same too, but I can't verify that. It's not something I would normally choose, but right now I don't care.

As the young Jocks eat, the banter begins; they are getting restless. Ptes Ferris and Duffy are joking, taking the piss out of each other. Ferris blows kisses to the blokes on other wagons and makes obscene gestures around his groin area, all whilst manning his .50-cal. machine gun. The young Jocks fall about laughing; this is the norm around here, and Ferris's antics are a welcome break.

Ferris has managed to take my mind off my itchy wrists, which are starting to bother me. I have a rash caused by the fibreglass on top of the Land Rover; it slowly gets under your skin. Sitting back with my food and a cup of tea, my mind drifts off.

I start thinking about my time in army basic training, when I was always hungry, always drained. As recruit Taylor, I constantly wondered when the instructors or section commanders would finally stop beasting us – when they would feel they had subjected us to sufficient degradation.

Every day, I became mentally stronger. The army takes away your dignity, and you're not exactly sure what it is that they give back in return. That doesn't become clear until much later.

I was twenty-two years old when I enlisted. The youngest of five children, I was born in the south of England. I'd had a taste of life outside, having worked in the retail industry since leaving school. I started as part of the old youth training scheme, and at the age of just eighteen years, I managed my own concession. I excelled at the visual merchandising aspect and was often rewarded for my efforts with trips on shop refit tasks up and down the country. I travelled as far north as Manchester. Being away from home and on my own was initially daunting, but I eventually started to enjoy the independent feeling it gave me.

My glory was short-lived, and the trips away came to an abrupt end after my hotel bar bill far exceeded what it should have. This pushed me one step closer to my decision to join the army.

Growing up in the 1990s wasn't without its problems; there were a lot of distractions for young boys and girls. The country was still angry about hard decisions made to decide how we would move forward economically. Ecstasy and the 'Mad-Chester' drug culture were rife, and along with everyone else, I got caught up in the glamour of it all. I would sometimes hide out in my bedroom, listening endlessly to the Stone Roses' 'Waterfall' whilst puffing on a bong. I inhaled as if my life depended on it. Those were some of the darkest days of my life. Smoking marijuana did not suit my personality. I became withdrawn and paranoid, spending three months sponging off the state. I recall times when I was so stoned that I couldn't even be bothered to make the short walk to sign on for my 'free' money.

Gang violence, along with the football hooligan culture, was also prevalent. A sense of belonging to anything other than further education somehow made an awkward adolescence bearable. I had enrolled at my local college, with dreams of studying business law. Suffice to say that smoking weed all day came in really useful! I couldn't concentrate, and I struggled to remember what day it was – much less be able to study. It's fair to say that I dabbled with a life in 'shitsville', and I didn't like it. Escaping it made me mentally tough, and I somehow managed to drag my sorry arse to the army careers office, kicking and screaming all the way.

Every council estate or housing scheme across the UK is a 'target rich' recruiting area for the other ranks of the British military. Most soldiers hail from deprived areas, and that's no bad thing. I was ambitious, without being sure where I was going, and inquisitive about everything, without being sure what it was that I wanted to know. All the doubt and arrogance was soon drummed out of me during the unknown number of hours I spent on my belt buckle, crawling through mud and cow shit.

More often than not, I was running up and down the quarry hills. We had the luxury of physical training instructors who also trained the young guys who wanted to be paratroopers. You would never push yourself as hard or as far as the army pushes you. You stop thinking like a civilian and start thinking like a soldier. I had grown up on a council estate, believing like an idiot that skipping off school was clever; it wasn't. The bravado that I engaged in as a teenager just camouflaged my lack of confidence.

I was definitely looking for something other than the humdrum of a conventional job. I went through the mind-numbing day-in, day-out drills and instruction in a daze. In the end, I wanted nothing in return. I came to see that becoming a soldier had taken me into a world where I could make my mark. I'd grown an inch taller by straightening my backbone, and I no longer lacked confidence. That lack is the curse of the working class. I was interested in everything. I opted to become a combat medic technician (CMT). The word *combat* did not appear in the descriptions of any other jobs open to females back then, and that was the reason why I chose to become a CMT. That may sound crazy to people, just as it does to me now. I laugh to myself as I recall it.

In the next instant, my daydreaming ends, interrupted by the order to 'mount up' on the vehicles. Remnants of my tea cast away, I quickly jump up, helmet back on, chinstrap fastened.

The engines are running, and we are on the move again. It's late; the orange sunset lasts only seconds as we are cast into twilight. Night vision goggles (NVGs) are fitted, and night discipline begins. Orders have come from higher: we are heading into the smoke and gunfire around the district centre of Nad-e Ali.

My initial impression of atmospherics here are grim – plastic bags skipping down empty streets, that feeling of the calm before the storm. Everyone in the company feels it. They've got the look that Olympic high jumpers have before they sprint for the bar: determined and fully alert. It's 'game on', just as Kev noted earlier. Anticipation is sometimes worse than the actual event. You never know when or where it's going to happen. One thing that I am sure of is that I don't want it to be our wagon getting the good news first.

Flushed with adrenaline, I am no longer tired. I check that my medical kit is good to go. I forget my hunger, feeling relieved that I don't have to finish my cat food – not yet, anyway. We push on, making our way into what looks like a derelict school. It has been taken over by the headquarters (HQ) of an Afghan National Army (ANA) *kandak* (kandak means 'battalion' in Dari; roughly six hundred soldiers). They've taken several hits and are heavily undermanned. They would be lucky to count forty blokes, let alone six hundred.

Half the vehicles with Monty's platoon turn into the entrance of the walled yard. A group of Afghan soldiers stand about, their expressions hard to read. Monty's crew will spend the night here, showing the Afghans that we are willing to stand shoulder to shoulder with them.

The kandak is commanded by Lt Col Nazim, a tough-looking, battle-hardened veteran who fought with the mujahideen many years ago against the Russians. With Maj. Clark, Scotty McFadden, and the remainder of B Company, I press on to the Afghan National Police (ANP) compound, a sand-bricked building built around a courtyard in the centre of Nad-e Ali.

Travelling with our platoon is a Ford Ranger pickup packed with Afghan police. They hang on to the sides of the wagon with one hand, as the other holds a rocket propelled grenade (RPG) launcher, with one finger precariously curled round the trigger – a weird combination that filled me with dread. This isn't how we do it; your finger stays off the trigger until you are engaging something. Still, that's why we're here: to stimulate democracy, to teach the fledgling Afghan police and military the joys of battle discipline.

Once inside the compound, our wagons line up close to the wall. As soon as we go firm, LCpl Sean Maloney, unclipping his chinstrap, hurries across from his vehicle.

'Hey, it's Coaksee... he sick,' he says.

'What?' I reply.

'Coaksee, he sick with stomach. He look like shit.'

Pte Coakse ('Coaksee') is your stereotypical young Jock, too proud to admit he needs help. Sick or not, he's still able to smoke a cigarette.

'No dramas, Sean,' I say. 'I'll be over in a minute.'

In spite of his Irish name, Sean is from the Caribbean and has developed the look and persona of the rapper Dizzee Rascal. This helps his pursuit of the ladies, he claims. With his gangsta jargon, there are times when I think I need an interpreter in order to understand him, whereas I understand the Jocks' Scottish pronunciation perfectly because my mum is Irish born and was raised in Glasgow, Scotland.

However, having trained as an infantry soldier before becoming a combat medic, I know that Sean has a lot to offer in times of trouble. The Jocks are cutting about, checking weapons. Some push up onto the roof for better eyes on the surrounding area. I watch the Afghan police from our convoy jump out of their wagons. They look disinterested and shot to shit. To them, this is just another day in Helmand Province. Meanwhile, Scotty McFadden and the boss are holding an impromptu meeting with the other unit commanders.

I eventually find Coaksee gritting his teeth and leaning up against his WMIK. As Sean had so eloquently described, he looks like shit. I know straight away that he's embarrassed about needing attention.

'Alright,' he says with a grimace.

As I pause for thought, from nowhere someone screams: 'Incoming! Incoming!' The pre-impact *whoosh* is heard. Before I can reply to Coaksee, I'm scrambling around on the floor in the dark. Everyone's shouting; noise comes from all directions.

My head feels fuzzy, and the voices sound far away. For a moment I can't understand a thing. Welcome to the world of battle shock: it doesn't normally last long, but in some it may last a lifetime. I've been in contact before, and when it kicks off, you're always shocked, numb for a moment, disorientated. I check myself: limbs are intact, so I am happy to move off.

More explosions immediately slam into the base as RPGs rain down on us. They're coming in from two sides. You feel the thud before you hear it; the explosions drill into your ears and rattle your brain a little. A cloud of broken bricks and dust fills my immediate air space; I can taste it. Another RPG drills into the wall opposite. I'm pinned down with Sean and Coaksee behind one of the wheels on the WMIK. The three of us have managed to cram ourselves into a space no bigger than your average truck wheel. I like my own personal space and do not encourage others into it unless invited. None of us were asking for permission that day. I take hold of Coaksee's arm, and the three of us scramble to get into the hardened part of the compound.

I watch in disbelief as Maj. Clark and Scotty McFadden dodge their way across the open ground and climb the broken set of steps to the flat roof; they are open to enemy fire as they climb, and the steps are already shot to pieces. There goes that stupidity/bravery again. It's an uncontrollable, instantaneous reaction to combat, and your mindset makes the decision for you. On the roof they try to control the outgoing fire, and within seconds they've organised the ramshackle Afghan police who are engaging the enemy. Behind the rattle of our guns, I can hear the deep-throated roar of the Soviet-made DShK, a 12.7 mm heavy machine gun. It's the Taliban's most-ruthless weapon; for me, it is the stuff of nightmares. If I wasn't sure before, the atmospherics in this town tell me that Nad-e Ali is on its arse.

Rounds from semi-automatic weapons stitch holes into the walls. Flashes of electric-blue and -green light made by the blasts illuminate the faces of two of the Afghan police who have taken cover with us in the building. They have blank, exhausted eyes. Our enemies are Afghans, and the men sitting opposite are Afghans. There's no war like a civil war. We're outsiders, observers. We, like many before us, will leave our blood in the sand, and yet, one day we'll be going home. They, on the other hand, will remain here, and they will still have the same tribal conflicts they had long before the coalition arrived.

As for Coaksee, it's amazing what a shot of natural adrenaline can do for you. It draws out a peculiar energy. You face death and then suddenly feel reborn. The colour is back in his cheeks, and he joins the other blokes outside. My mind works overtime calculating how many casualties I think we are going to have, and, if my calculations are correct, we're fucked.

The barrage suddenly stops as I struggle to my feet. It didn't make sense. Either the Taliban had grown bored, or they had gone to ground after receiving the good news from our guns on the roof. Checking the guys around the lower part of the compound, I search for casualties. I am shocked to learn that by some miracle we haven't sustained any. I don't ponder on what might have been; the result is definitely favourable, and I am grateful. A medic's life is different from that of any other type of soldier: we train and train, scenario after scenario, but every casualty is unique, and a feeling of dread always comes over me before I reach our injured. Being in the spotlight in these circumstances can make for a very lonely existence. I zip around the compound before making my way up the steps onto the roof.

Searching for the boss, I find him sitting behind a small brick wall, relaying communications to brigade HQ through Kev. His eyes are bright in the dim light, and dirt and dust cover his cheeks.

'We're good, sir. No casualties,' I say.

He returns a rare smile, saying simply, 'Thanks, Sgt T.'

I nod, not at all surprised by his brief response. Maj. Harry Clark is in his thirties, a tall man with sculptured features. He is well-educated and resolute, an officer with a stiff upper lip that never falters. He is passionate about his regiment and always thinks before he speaks.

At that same moment, Monty's tobacco-thickened voice comes on the radio net from the old school, the first place we stopped to give support to the kandak that are housed there. There is a quick exchange of call signs.

Monty says, 'Advice needed from M1.' Mike one is my call sign as lead medic.

'My medic has four cat-B casualties.'

Cat-B signifies that the casualties require urgent surgery.

Four cat-Bs, even for an experienced medic, could prove overwhelming.

'How's she doing?' I ask quickly, referring to the medic.

'Best she can,' he says. 'She's worked on three. No breath sounds on one side of the fourth. You happy if she decompresses his chest?'

'Roger that,' I reply.

'She wants clearance,' he adds.

We have no doctor here. I am the buffer for my medics, and, should she need help, I am a kilometre away.

'Go ahead,' is my response.

'Roger that. Out.'

This is a baptism of fire for Pte Abbie Cottle, a slim, attractive brunette. Abbie is very calm around casualties and has a methodical approach to problem solving; she has the ideal temperament and is well suited to life as a combat medic. She hails from Gloucester and embraces the twang of a southern accent.

She reminds me of what it was like to be a junior medic – when you know the answers but lack the confidence and years of experience to make 'that' call. Even now, I check in for a second opinion; you never stop learning when it comes to medicine. The moment that you stop asking is the time to look at a different career.

I have already come to rely heavily on Abbie this tour. She has chosen Helmand as her first operational deployment, which is not a bad start if you want to get bloodied early.

'Sir, these guys will need to be evacuated,' I advise the OC.

Maj. Clark has been following the conversation, and he gives Kev Coyle the nod. In turn, Kev gets on the net to brigade HQ at Lashkar Gah, giving them a casualty report. We soon get the order to transport the injured to a helicopter landing zone

(HLZ) outside of Nad-e Ali. It would be less detrimental for the injured men to bring the aircraft nearer to the old school, but it is deemed too risky for the pilots to land in an unknown area of operations (AO).

'Sir, are you happy if I take LCpl Young with me?' I ask.

'Yes, do,' he replies.

The boss always accommodates his medics, allowing us the freedom to crack on with our tasks with little interference. Our working relationship has been built through trust and sound judgement. It wasn't always this easy.

The steps down to the compound are thick with dust, and in my haste I slip, making sure to catch my tail bone on the edge of the step. I stand up, swiftly dusting myself off.

Jenny Young is waiting at the bottom of the stairs; as usual, she is good to go before my even telling her that she is needed.

'Jen, you are coming with me. We're going back to the old school to evacuate these four casualties,' I say.

LCpl Jenny Young is the third member of my team, a tall redhead whose resilience and strength never cease to amaze me. She is quiet in character, an old-school Northerner who only speaks if she has something intelligent to say. She doesn't waffle and just cracks on with the task in hand. We were here together back in 2006. Jen was a medic on the blue-light matrix, fetching casualties from helicopters and transporting our dead and wounded to the hospital in Camp Bastion.

We're taking two WMIK Land Rovers back to the ANA base. Instinctively, I climb into the vehicle with the biggest weapon – a .50-cal. machine gun – with Pte Michael Duffy cleaning dust off the barrel. The stuff is everywhere, thick as snow across the compound. It is just like talcum powder, getting into everything – up your nose, between the gaps in your teeth, in the corners of your eyes.

'You know how to work that thing, Duffy?' I ask.

'Aye, you having a fuckin' laugh?' he says.

Laughing at Duffy's response, I explain, 'Four casualties at the school. We're moving them out to an HLZ a couple of clicks away.'

'Ne dramas, mucker,' he replies.

Duffy is tall and slim; he has a runner's build. He is clean-shaven and not growing a beard any time soon, on account of barely being out of short trousers. I remember Duffy from Lash, when he was an eighteen-year-old arsehole who listened to hardcore rave music and drank too much Red Bull. He was a loud, irritating kid. That was twelve hours ago. By magic or some conjurer's trick, that irritating teenager has turned into someone else. I now look at Duffy in a very different light.

Like me, Mike Duffy could have taken a very different path in life. He could have hung around on street corners, feeling cheated and believing that the world somehow owed him a living. Instead he chose to serve his country, and now he was protecting me and my casualties. People have paths to follow in life, and they each choose different ones for different reasons. Duffy and I might be almost a generation apart in age, but in this situation we fit perfectly. Life sometimes places you exactly where you should be, for good or bad.

The engine starts up, and we head off beneath the eerie light of the stars. My legs feel like jelly.

The Taliban are out there, sons of the sons of the same resolute fighters that have always been there. They say Afghanistan is the 'graveyard of empires'. The Afghans routed the Russians, and the tribes kept us Brits from planting the Union Jack over Kabul. In the third century BC, Alexander the Great lost half his army in four years of battle, only sealing the peace by marrying Roxana, daughter of a Bactrian named Oxyartes of Balkh (in Bactria, then the eastern Achaemenid Empire, now northern Afghanistan, Uzbekistan, and Tajikistan). She married Alexander at the age of sixteen years, after he visited the fortress of Sogdian Rock. Balkh was the last of the Persian Empire's provinces to fall to Alexander. Like most soldiers, I started to read about the history of the place before we deployed. History was now telling me that everything we are doing here has been done before, and whatever mistakes were made back then, we are making again.

Small-arms fire rumbles through the night as we make the short trip to pick up the casualties. The Land Rovers which we are travelling in don't have sufficient under armour to deflect the huge blasts caused by well-placed bombs. Any insurgent looking at tracks on a road can judge the route that a driver will take on any given day. While we've been pinned down in the compound, the Taliban may have sown the road with IEDs. In the dark it is harder to make out abnormal ground sign; it's a good indicator that enemy have been active. Every metre, every minute, seems to take longer than normal.

'You're quiet, Channy,' Duffy says. I don't reply, for some reason thinking that he is talking to someone else, but he soon gets my attention. 'Fuck me, it's the morale police!' he shouts.

Duffy's banter reminds me not to dwell too much on our situation, and my mood immediately brightens. He slaps the barrel on his .50 cal. 'I'm getting paid for this shite,' he says. At eighteen, Duffy has no fear.

The roads are deserted except for some scrawny dogs that stand as still as statues, watching the vehicles pass. We make it to the kandak base without incident.

It's good to see Monty and to hear his Jock welcome. 'Yous lot took yur fuckin' time!'

This is a good sign: some salty language means morale is

okay. Soldiers survive on banter; it takes their minds off the fact that they, like the four casualties, might be in a world of pain at any moment. Once you are accepted into the fold, you can expect insults involving family members, including suggestions that your mother is doing something unmentionable.

Through an opening in the door I get a glimpse of Abbie at the centre of a group of Afghan soldiers. I follow Monty through to the group. The moment he speaks, other conversations end. Monty has blue-grey eyes like chips of flint, and a presence that leaves no doubt as to who's in charge. 'I've been keeping my eye on her,' he whispers. 'She's done well, mate.'

As I enter the room where Abbie has been working, the smell of gasoline, human shit, and the cold coppery tang of blood hits me. The four wounded are all Afghans. Two have chest injuries, and two have multiple shrapnel and fragmentation wounds. The five Afghans helping out as medical orderlies have lowered eyes and expressions that are both respectful and bewildered. This could well be their first encounter with a Western woman. Maybe they've never seen the face of any woman except their mother, and the way they are willingly taking instructions from Abbie is a positive sign. They say in Afghanistan that a woman should only leave her home twice in her life: the first time when she abandons her father's house to marry, and the second when she is taken from her husband's house to be buried.

Abbie's drawn features tell me all about the kind of night she's been having. I move among the casualties, checking that they are stable enough to fly. She has kept four men alive in a situation that would have tested anyone. Although junior in years and rank, she remains calm under pressure. She was the first medic on scene after an IED killed Cpl Sarah Bryant, along with three special operations reserve soldiers, just weeks ago.

My mind drifts back to the details of that situation. I recall being very puzzled by the attitude of brigade staff after that hideous incident. News came through that we had lost four individuals, including one female. Naturally, my first thoughts were of Abbie and Jen, as my two medics were both out on the ground, one with the stricken call sign. Sadly, Sarah lost her life along with three operators, Sean, Richie, and Paul. Abbie, along with the remainder of the patrol, was tasked to cordon off and guard the scene through the night. The following morning at breakfast, I was informed that all female soldiers on site were to report to the cookhouse at 0930 hours for a 'lines to take' briefing, with reference to the heavy media presence on base. I took along my notebook and pen and waited patiently, sitting on the tables outside the main dining hall, keeping myself under the canvas for shade. There were about eight other females in attendance. Some who had shared accommodation with Sarah were visibly distraught.

The incident reminded us all that the Taliban weren't discriminating when planning their attacks. They hit the propaganda jackpot by killing a pretty young blonde female – or at least we as a nation allowed them to hit that jackpot. Out of the blue, brigade commander Brig. Carlton-Smith appeared. Taken aback, I wondered why he, such a high-ranking commander, was giving us a 'lines to take' briefing; this was normally a task for the media operations cell. I asked the captain sitting to my left if she knew what was going on, but she appeared to be as confused as I was. It didn't take long for all to become clear.

Bracing up as he arrived at the table, his voice softened as he told us to relax. Then came the impromptu counselling session, covering the effect on the entirety of the base and the emotional turmoil that we as women might feel. He went on to explain that it could be very difficult emotionally for us to lose one of our own.

Furious, I began to rage inside. The brigade commander had spent most of his career in an all-male environment. Knowing that, I tried to imagine, or at least understand, where all of this was leading. Sarah died serving as a soldier on the front line; she had earned the very basic right to be treated as a front-line soldier, she'd made the ultimate sacrifice for her country.

With the brief coming to an awkward end, we were asked to offer up any additional points. I looked around the table in search of support, none visible my hand shot up as soon as the commander's final sentence finished. He looked straight at me. 'Sir, should anyone at this table be asked about their feelings or opinions on this, can we remember that three blokes died yesterday as well?' I stopped there, as I could feel his eyes boring into me, but I had looked directly at him the entire time, and I had spoken in a clear, unfaltering tone.

He replied, 'Yes, good point.'

It was the only point. We should never have been sitting there, and he knew it. If I could have said what I was really thinking, the conversation would have started with, 'If someone with ginger hair dies, are you going to call in everyone with ginger hair for a debriefing?' I could understand if we were a platoon or company group, but none of us even worked together.

My better judgement stopped the ginger comment from ever crossing the threshold of my mouth. I was very sad to lose Sarah, but I was as equally sad about Sean, Richie, and Paul. Any loss of life bears the same amount of grief, and we all know that a family will be suffering at home regardless of sex, colour, or religion.

Our media have a habit of making one life seem more important than the next. Misogyny is rife throughout the ranks of any military. It so often devalues the hard work that female soldiers put in. In many arenas, women are mentally stronger than men. I absolutely understand that not all places are designed for all women. On the flipside of that, however is that some places are not designed for all men. I have encountered plenty who don't meet to the mark; luckily for them, though, they hide among the majority. I have sometimes sold myself short in a male-dominated environment, as it's all too easy to think as an individual and try to succeed alone. If you take nine guys and one woman, put them in a room, and run a weapon handling lesson, who are your eyes drawn to? Your eyes are drawn to the woman because it is human nature to look at the one who is different. I learnt an easy lesson there: become more qualified than your peers, and grow a thick skin. Choosing a life that is less than ordinary is never going to be easy, and the struggle is the interesting part.

Afghan commander Nazim appears, bringing my mental meanderings to a halt. His face stern and patrician below his green beret, he says a few words in Dari and then squeezes the shoulders of each of his injured men before we carry them out on makeshift stretchers to the wagons. 'Thank you, Sergeant,' he says to Monty. He turns, bowing his head just slightly to Abbie. 'Thank you.' The fleeting moment shared by the former mujahideen warrior and the young Englishwoman is oddly moving. It brings into focus the reason why we're here.

The moment passes, and I brief Abbie on the move. 'Stay with him, Abs,' I say, pointing to the least stable of the four. 'We will sort out the rest.' My inner thought is that the casualty will be lucky to make the journey, but that remains just a thought.

The Jocks and Afghan soldiers cautiously place the stretchers on the wide floor space in the wagons. Battlefield wounds are hard to deal with at the best of times, and this is all the more difficult when evacuating across rough ground. We make our wounded comfortable and carry out essential drills, checking that tourniquets are secure and intravenous (IV) drips are locked in place.

Army training teaches you that the whole is greater than the parts. Afghan men are proud of their individuality, and they mark it with the way they arrange their lungee (headwear) and shoulder their weapons. They have different methods, and we try to work around some of their less-practical drills by guiding them away from killing themselves through negligence or lack of education. We set off in a four-wagon convoy, past the hungry dogs, and out on to the pitch-black road that runs along the side of the canal next to the old school.

I smoke a cigarette, trying to keep myself focused. An occasional smoker, I promise myself that I will quit tomorrow, remembering that I made the same promise on my last tour of Helmand when I was supporting 3rd Battalion, the Parachute Regiment (3 PARA), working long gruelling hours at the hospital in Camp Bastion. The medical facility was then one of the few permanent structures in a sprawling camp of blast blocks, T-walls, and razor wire carved out of the wilderness in what the locals call the 'Desert of Death'. Our surgeons, nurses, and the National Health Service (NHS) volunteers were pioneering new techniques and saving more lives than ever, as the insurgency gathered pace back in the summer of 2006. Two years later, it is hard to see any progress in Afghanistan, and in some cases we are moving backwards.

The moon is high tonight, offering a fair degree of light to outline the tall vegetation running alongside the canal. Ten minutes pass, and we're at the HLZ. The drivers kill the engines.

I step out of the vehicle, wondering which way the helicopter is going to land. Is the doctor going to come off? Do they want the casualties on head or feet first? Medics are always worrying and listing problems, hoping for the best and expecting the worst. My eyes are strained from looking through the NVG for so long. I should know to blink more often.

'Helo inbound!' Monty relays communications as he joins me.

Through the shadows I can see Abbie kneeling by her casualty. I get eyes on the Chinook's glimmering rotor blades. I hear the sound, the familiar *whomph, whomph*, the chug of the big engines.

The Chinook is an essential piece of kit for any war fighting army, and I never stop being surprised that we have so few of them. Cylums (or chemical lights) illuminate the ground. The blokes grab for the stretcher handles. The helicopter hovers above as it slows before settling down, the blades whipping up a storm. Wincing as the grainy sand and grit scratches my exposed lower back, I realise an instant too late that I have forgotten to tuck my shirt in.

The Chinook doesn't hang around. We load up our injured, opting for head first. The team receiving nod their heads before giving a thumbs up as I hand over the paperwork. It's all done in less than thirty seconds, and the four injured Afghan soldiers are whisked away, back to the trauma unit in Camp Bastion.

Standing next to Monty, I put my thoughts into words. 'I should have asked if they were carrying any spare stretchers.'

His brow crinkles. 'Yeah, we are going to need them.'

I turn to face him. 'Yeah, right. We'll be back in Lash tomorrow.'

He looks like he knows something that I don't. 'We're going to be stuck here for a wee while yet, mate,' he says.

The move back to the district centre of Nad-e Ali has everyone on edge. Using the same routes in and out of any hostile area makes our call sign vulnerable to an enemy ambush.

Rubbing my hand across my lower back now, I feel the raw

open grazes that were a gift of my inability to tuck my shirt in during the casualty extraction. It's a minor injury, but as my Osprey body armour gets to work on it, the pain is ever present. I return to the task.

The move back goes by without incident. We roll into the old school, which by now is bathed in light only from the high moon. I catch a quick word with Monty before the remainder of us push on to the police station in the district centre.

'Stay safe, mucker,' he says. 'I'll catch yous lot the morra.'

Our two vehicles press on, and my watch is telling me that I need sleep. Today feels like it is never going to end.

The police station is in darkness, and the only sound is the noise coming from the engines of our vehicles.

Duffy dismounts from his position on the .50 calibre. 'I'm fucked,' he grunts.

I am too tired to offer any response, and my body aches from being crammed in the back of the vehicle. I feel my soaked shirt under my body armour, and lap up the smell of dried blood. Jumping down from the tailgate, I grab my kit, slinging my weapon on my back.

Scrambling up the dusty, barely there steps and onto the roof, I make my way over to check in with Maj. Clark.

He acknowledges my return. 'Everything alright, Sgt T?'

'All good, sir. Everything went smoothly.'

Almost but never quite forgetting the deep grazes now covering the lumbar region of my lower back, I find a darkened corner to strip off some clothing. Being culturally aware is a lifesaver out here. Taking some gauze, I soak it with saline solution to clean the initial bloody mess. The application of an antiseptic solution gets a bit emotional; medics don't make good patients. Dressing applied, I emerge from the shadows and look for a space to settle down for a few hours. There are bodies strewn all over the roof, it's cold, and there is very little shelter. It's exposed to the fresh winds coming in from the open desert a few kilometres north of Nad-e Ali.

The town sits in the west of Helmand Province. Much of the district is unoccupied desert, with the bulk of population living in the east, near the provincial capital of Lashkar Gah. This district thrives on its opium trade, with a high percentage of the profits going directly to officials in Kabul. The local people are not overly supportive of the coalition; they know that it's only a matter of time before we leave.

Still searching for somewhere to sleep, I spot our interpreter sleeping soundly in his bulky army-issue sleeping bag. He has sensibly packed the 'bouncing bomb'. It is a huge piece of kit given out back in the UK. It's rarely used by troops because of its unmanageable size: it can easily fill a bergen (backpack).

I left my sleeping bag behind, quite sensibly, I thought at the time. When packing my kit, I opted for my bivvy bag, which is basically a protective outer layer or shell for the proper sleeping bag. It is thin and offers little comfort, and, yes, I am now regretting my decision. Mumbling with discontent, I climb into my bivvy and try to get comfortable, but my overtired brain keeps me awake. I suffer a further hour of the cold and a series of 'what if this happens or that happens' before deciding to adopt the spoons position behind our interpreter. This will at least afford me some of his body heat. He's asleep and doesn't realise that I am there. When he wakes, he will presume that it's one of the blokes, and for that reason alone, he won't be too bothered. What's left of the cold night flashes by.

At dawn, we stand to. When first light comes, it is usually accompanied by some form of attack; the Taliban have had the night to manoeuvre and plan what will be another day's paid work for them. Briefs given prior to deployment cover a range of interesting facts and figures that are only put into perspective when you end up in a patrol base (PB) or forward operating base (FOB). Payment includes ten dollars a day and as much opium as you can handle while remaining marginally coherent. The going rate for local young men to join the fight against the infidels has proven too good an offer to turn down.

As quick as the landscape is exposed by the sun, my attempts to stay warm offer the soldiers around me some much-needed laughter and a morale boost.

Kev is the first to applaud my resourcefulness. 'Smooth operator, mucker! Ne flies on you, eh?' he says.

'Aye, Kev, am shocked you weren't in the bag wi' him, ya wee fanny,' Scotty McFadden joins in the banter.

'Not sure if Ryan would appreciate you dating our interpreter, Channy,' Jen joins in the banter.

Ryan is my fiancé. He serves as part of a fire support group (FSG) within 3 PARA. We met back in 2005, in our local pub at home. He is upcountry working as part of the over watch for the Kajaki turbine move. We have no means of communication here, so I try to leave any thoughts of missing him alone. On our last tour, I wrote him a letter every day during my shift in the hospital at Camp Bastion. He was in the Sangin Valley then, during the very worst fighting of 2006.

Our jovialities and my reminiscences come to an end as Jocks to the left of me have eyes on a group of fighting-age males fewer than two hundred yards from the base. Normally not seen as an issue in a densely populated area, the group is out of sync. Abnormal activity in a place that has been under attack for more than three weeks classifies the men as hostile; no weapons have been identified, so they aren't engaged. They are followed, and grids are marked, along with timings and descriptions.

Logging any type of suspected enemy activity is important;

it builds a picture of what is an unknown AO, and intelligence gathering will identify how they move and the types of numbers that they move in.

The group of males disappears into a tree line; teams on the roof will continue to monitor them, allowing the rest of the young Jocks to get busy cleaning weapons and preparing themselves for the day ahead. Boil-in-the-bag rations are eaten cold, and I tuck into my cat food and biscuits, which up until now I had managed to avoid.

It's not long before Monty joins us from the old school. He undertakes a vital role within B Company, and heads straight to Maj. Clark for orders. Scotty and the Sgt Maj. are also in attendance as our mission changes. Our trip back to the relative luxury of Lashkar Gah is no longer happening, so the forty-eight-hour operation has become a thing of the past. 'We will move as a call sign complete to the old school, enabling support to what is left of the kandak. We will remain there and conduct operations to flush out the Taliban of Nad-e Ali until further notice.' Maj. Clark breaks this news to team commanders, who in turn pass the good news to the blokes in their sections.

I gather my medics, and we talk about the basic set-up of a company aid post (CAP); we will sort ourselves out when we get to the school.

Looking at Kev with half a smile, I sort my equipment out and make some notes about the medical supplies we are going to need. Before leaving, Monty notices one of the junior officers, 2Lt Barclay, has placed a belt of ammunition upside down onto one of the machine guns. Barclay would later be awarded the Military Cross for bravery, but now he is verbally chastised to the delight of the junior Jocks, five or more of them making the squawking sound of a crow.

The area housing the vehicles is a hive of activity. Wagons

are squared away, and B Company is preparing to move. Young Duffy is busy checking his much-loved .50 cal., and I take time to dust off and battle clean my own weapon, checking my medical kit before mounting up with Kev and Maj. Clark. Our interpreter looks the least happy about staying out for longer than expected; not everyone on this mission has that glint in their eye.

'Cpl Coyle, are we good to go?' the boss asks.

'Roger that, sir,' Kev replies, giving his usual wry smile.

We set off towards our new home, the sound of muffled small-arms fire in the background. This would turn out to be the least kinetic move that we would experience over the next two months.

CHAPTER 2

ESTABLISH ROUTINE

B COMPANY ARRIVES AT THE AFGHAN BASE JUST BEFORE midday. The place looks different from what I could recollect from yesterday. It was shabby and makeshift, displaying all the scars of a base under siege. Afghan soldiers sit around, some smoking, some chatting, and others sleeping. They look crushed, and we are quickly informed that they have been getting smashed by the Taliban for several weeks, constantly engaged in close-quarter firefights. They have lost several men and are low on food and ammunition. Hand-to-hand combat has left many dejected, and their battle-worn faces say it all.

This kandak fights alone and unsupported, and they have no indirect fire weapons, such as artillery; nor are they afforded the luxury of CAS in the form of Apaches or fixed wing fighter aircraft that coalition forces can call upon.

These men are fierce and proud fighters, although many lack the basic discipline that Western soldiers learn in training. Weapons and equipment must be looked after if they are to survive the intemperate conditions of Helmand. However, the Afghans are in disarray, and their battle discipline is non-existent. Their body armour is all over the place – weapons leant up against walls in direct sunlight, rubbish strewn everywhere. They have been using the outer wall as a toilet, and the smell of human faecal matter is so strong that it overpowers the diesel fumes from our vehicles.

Davey Robertson, B Company's sergeant major, sets about 'claiming' some real estate so his men can establish a routine. He is an old-school soldier with a strong character, and by all accounts he is a bit of a 'hard cunt', as so delicately described by his men. I have yet to see any takers put this to the test. Just under six feet tall, Davey is covered in old tattoos. He has a glint in his eye, just like my man Duffy. Davey's happy hardcore music would have probably been the Jam or AC/DC. That's how it works: generations may change, but we all had our struggles somewhere along the line. It's called 'common ground', and it's how people in the military get on. You may not like the guy standing next to you, but you will find common ground with him in order to ensure that the job gets done. Beyond that, a mutual respect grows out of displayed skill and time spent together. I have only ever seen that in the military, and, more often than not, you grow to like someone's once-annoying habits.

Monty and Scotty get busy placing troops into defensive positions ensuring all arcs – where the Taliban might attack from – are covered. (The idea behind this is that our PB will have all-round defence should the Taliban mount an assault.)

An ANA position on the roof of the tallest building is reinforced with a heavy machine gun. When troops are not on patrol, the big .50-calibre guns can be dismounted from vehicles and placed where they can be used most effectively. This job is left in the capable hands of young section commander Cpl Scotty Pew. Pew's section has the back-breaking job of carrying sandbags up onto the roof to reinforce the gun position. This is both a physically demanding and time-consuming job. Sandbags are filled before Pew and his men carry them one by one up the dodgy steps and onto the roof; the steps are riddled with 7.62mm holes from earlier clashes with the enemy.

The Taliban would have eyes on the position at all times. Pew and the other young Jocks were happy that the enemy knew they were there. For them, it meant that the Taliban could see the firepower that would smash them in any future attack.

Pte Drew Elder is another young soldier busy on the roof. Elder issued fire control orders last night to the less-experienced Jocks, acting as platoon runner for Scotty McFadden. Relaying information from one area of the roof to another, Elder took on the role of 'link man' for the platoon. The link man is probably the most important job in any fighting unit: if Elder gets it wrong the platoon, even the entire company, will become combat ineffective very quickly. Elder was raised in Falkirk, and he's learning fast that his job is a thankless and sometimes perilous task. He puts his life on the line with every step taken in his role as link man.

Every soldier has a job to complete before any contemplation of rest is realised. Maj. Clark's communications (comms) are set up by Kev, who quickly turns an unused classroom into our command post (CP). Kev has the unenviable chore of keeping this company in comms with brigade HQ.

Stopping my own job of setting up a CAP, I take a short break for a much-needed drink of water. I look around at the young soldiers going about their business, and it suddenly dawns on me that not so long ago some of them would have been bumming around Glasgow or other cities, sipping from bottles of tonic wine. They would have gone through the same decisions that I did before signing up.

Many are from broken homes, or they crossed to and from

the wrong side of the tracks. Colourful backgrounds are in abundance throughout most armies. To me, this is nothing to be ashamed of; if anything, it develops character, and that is exactly what we need if we are to stand any chance of holding Nad-e Ali.

The young Jocks now man the corners of this isolated PB, poised to introduce the Taliban to a 'Glasgow kiss', in the shape of a .50-cal. machine gun. The only drink in sight is bottled water, or a few cans of Red Bull that the lads have managed to squeeze into their vehicles or bergens. When it comes to fighting, these men do it with ease; they are steeped in an infectious lust for life. Hardened beyond their years, their instinct to survive comes from a history of ferocious fighting men.

As I make my way back into the ops room, my team are busy emptying two patrol medical packs. We operate a military medical assessment using the MARCH-P principals:

M – Massive Haemorrhage

A – Airway

R – Respiratory/Chest

C – Circulation

H – Head Injury/Motor Function/Hypothermia

P – Pain/Environment/Evacuation

It differs from our civilian counterparts, as a massive haemorrhage will kill someone on the battlefield long before a blocked airway will. We use tourniquets far more freely in our line of work, and it would seem that the conflicts in Iraq,

Somalia, and Afghanistan are helping the medical world adopt new protocols when dealing with traumatic injuries.

As CMTs, we carry battlefield trauma bags and small primary health-care packs. Extensive training, followed by intensive live tissue scenarios, best prepares medics for the types of injuries seen in war. Using 'Amputees in Action' was a major boost for our brigade; we were the first to trial the system. The guys were a mixture of military and civilians. I was amazed that some of them were literally reliving the trauma that they had already been through; battle-simulation noises and smoke contributed to the realism of the scenarios. Medics not suited to the front-line role were sifted out during these tests. Some medics are great in a clinical environment but not comfortable in the field, so this method of testing ensured that the soldier on the ground received the very best treatment that we could provide. When the make-up artist is done with guys already missing limbs, they look and feel exactly like the real thing. Add to that some realistic pyrotechnics, and you have some of the most-realistic training to date. Panic, shock, and awe equate to only a fraction of how you will feel when an incident proper occurs. Having said that, nothing prepares you for your own reaction. I have come to believe that every incident is different, and it's always going to be the small things that get you flustered, or push you to 30,000 feet and rising. Mine is: 'Where the fuck are my gloves? I am sure they were in my pocket!'

I have three junior medics in my charge, so the two remaining patrol packs will be used when members of the trauma team deploy outside the wire. As lead medic, I answer to the boss, Maj. Harry Clark, and advise him on all matters concerning his men and their well-being.

There is no room for error in my role, but I am prepared. I was waiting for this my whole life. Could I deliver under pressure, or would self-doubt cripple me? Ultimately, could I live with the prospect of letting these men down? Anyone who puts their head above the pulpit will open up to the chance of failure.

I learnt early on to leave my ego at home. An overactive ego has a tendency to get people killed. The state of the world today, not to mention a fair number of battles throughout history, will tell you that. The British insist that everyone has the ability to step up if required. One moment, you are carrying out orders from higher command; the next, you are stepping up to deal with situations that far exceed your pay scale or rank.

I covered the medical desk in brigade HQ, a job usually taken on by a senior captain or major. On my first day, a mass casualty call came in: over thirty Afghans, including children, were ambushed by Taliban fighters as they travelled by bus out of one of the district centres. I had to quickly evaluate and decide what major air assets were required, and then I had to make the necessary arrangements for evacuation. Further complicating the situation was the fact that the injured were local nationals; some would come to our own location at Lash, some would be seen at Camp Bastion, and those with less-severe injuries would go to the local hospital in the district centre of the provincial capital (Lash).

My moment of truth played out under the watchful eye of the brigade commander; this was when I could do with a bit of his 'counselling'. The pressure I placed on myself was ridiculous, but I was determined to see it through. I did not falter. The assets required were multimillion-pound airframes carrying highly skilled teams. I wasn't about to start playing my own version of war gaming or Risk. I briefed the chief of staff on what the medical situation required, and he, as a lieutenant colonel, gave the final order to move. Airframes were allocated to task, and, eventually, all casualties were retrieved and in the hands of medical personnel. It took several hours to complete, but the end state was welcome – not necessarily for our wounded, of course, but at least they were no longer at the mercy of the Taliban.

The buzzing activity of the PB brings me back to the moment. The hours have passed, increasing the heat; that, combined with my overzealous start to the day, has left me hungry. I tuck into more of my ration-pack pâté and biscuits before making my way into the ops room to help Kev tape up the windows, using black bin liner bags to drown out any light. Light from the smallest source travels far, and drawing attention to the room could have disastrous consequences.

Sangin Valley, 2006: Effect from a light source travelling at night initiated a 107 mm enemy rocket attack, killing two British soldiers.

Basic battle discipline was the only way to survive here. The atmosphere around the base is one of trepidation. A structure opposite us and identical to our own houses the Afghan army; they look on inquisitively as we continue to turn the ramshackle base into a workable fortress in minimal time. My peripheral vision witnesses a flash of movement – a group of Afghan soldiers diving for cover – as I hear the initial crack of incoming rounds.

Taliban rounds slam into the base, punching small holes into the walls and sandbags. Kev sends the initial contact report, and already the heavy machine guns on the roof are letting rip, pounding the enemy positions. The sound is deafening, making it hard to tell the difference between outgoing and incoming fire. Monty and Scotty are directing our fire. Bursts from the .50-cal. guns stop only to allow the distinctive crack of the 7.62 mm GPMG or 240.

Amid the noise and chaos, the boss, Maj. Clark, tries hard

to control his men, issuing direct orders for the link man Elder to carry to the roof. Under heavy fire, Elder sprints off into the clouds of sand and broken brick thrown up by the rounds pumping into the buildings. He returns with news of what and who is being engaged from the roof. It appears that the fighting-age males noted earlier have returned, and they are now just south of their original position. It's hard to tell if they are the exact group; however, the grid and descriptions logged all point to that conclusion. This time they are armed, which now make them fair game.

Scotty Pew has eyes on ten or more enemy fighters: they are using the canal and compounds as cover, moving freely between tree lines and overgrown fields. His gun group engages them with several bursts from the .50 calibre. The rounds from this weapon system are the same size as a thick felt-tip pen or a large Sharpie – you don't want to be on the receiving end of 50-calibre fire.

Within ten minutes, five enemy fighters are confirmed dead. An Apache has arrived on station and is now stalking Taliban targets from the sky. This strange looking hi-tech helicopter has the profile of a mantis. The Apache is the biggest success story in Helmand. In military terms, it is a 'force multiplier', meaning that it can deliver the firepower of a support weapons company and more, with two air crew, a chain gun, and a pile of missiles. It's not long before the engagement starts to appear one sided. With no reports of friendly casualties, the balance has been tipped in our favour: nine Taliban are confirmed dead.

I take a sip of water during the lull in gunfire, and it would seem that all is well. Relaxing too soon, a blast pierces my ears, rattling every bone in my body. First, I see a flash, and soon I feel the shock wave from the explosion. It's close, far closer than I would like. Something has been hit. As I wait for more explosions, someone shouts, 'Incoming!'

Kev quickly follows this with, 'No fuckin' shit, Sherlock.' He looks across at me and gives the nod of approval that our taped-up window job has achieved its goal. No inward blast, luckily for Kev – it would have cut him in two in the spot where he sits relaying updates to brigade HQ.

A voice screams, 'Medic! Medic!' Whenever the dreaded call comes, it always sounds desperate. I instantly think, *Gloves?* A quick check confirms that they are in the pocket where I left them, so it's all good.

The base is in silence. Jen and I sprint out from our cover, almost colliding with the boss. He directs us to the outer wall where Cpl Tony McParland was firing from. The sweet smell of burnt carbon against the metal from the big guns on the roof forms a thick wall of smoke impairing each step. When multiple rounds are fired, you'd be forgiven for believing that you're just present at a fireworks display. The distinct smell is one that never leaves you.

It's a short distance to Tony, so we get there quickly. Stomach churning, I dread what we will find. As I said, no incident is ever the same, so our systematic approach to treatment must happen without delay. Tony's body is abnormally twisted, and I initially spot a mangled hand with fingers missing. Relieved that it is only fingers and not limbs, I take a deep breath. Like clockwork, our treatment begins. Already in enough cover so no movement is required, I talk through each section of MARCH-P in my head, making sure not to miss a single thing. My assessment takes less than sixty seconds, getting the all-important tourniquet applied to a heavy bleed on his left arm. It's care under fire, so the initial survey is super quick – we are just lucky enough to carry out any medical interventions at all. As the gunfire resumes, we drag Tony into the cover of the CAP.

Once there, our next move is to identify the need for early surgery. More often than not, injuries sustained on the battlefield require minimal first aid and super-quick evacuation to the hands of the highly skilled surgeons in Camp Bastion, the world's busiest trauma centre. No fingers are found on initial assessment and no lives are ever risked hunting for those fingers. Jen starts to dress his wounds before Tony can get eyes on them.

Noise from the guns engaging the enemy from above make it hard to concentrate, and the failing light offers up its own set of problems. I relay to Kev that we have at least one cat-B, which signifies that he is an urgent surgical case and has life-/limb-threatening injuries. The UK military have an established system to prioritise injuries into three groups, which indicate to everyone involved the urgency of the sustained injuries:

Cat-A – Life-threatening injuries, and the casualty requires urgent medical treatment.

Cat-B – Life-threatening injuries, and the casualty requires urgent surgical treatment.

Cat-C – Non-life-threatening injuries, and the casualty can be held for up to four hours.

Kev initiates a 'nine-liner' to HQ. This set of nine questions is answered by call signs on the ground and then sent up via the radio net to brigade HQ. These answers are then assessed at the medical desk, resulting in a decision which will see an instant response if relevant or a timely extraction, depending on the injury. This was the same call I received when I covered the desk; but now I am the one on the ground making the desperate call for support, a completely different perspective.

The nine-liner provides vital information to the chain of command, and all UK medical teams use it on operations:

Line 1: Location of the pick-up site.

Line 2: Radio frequency, call sign, and suffix.

Line 3: Number of patients, by precedence (cat-A, cat-B, or cat-C).

Line 4: Special equipment required.

Line 5: Number of patients by type (stretcher/walking wounded).

Line 6: Security at pick-up site.

Line 7: Method of marking pick-up site.

Line 8: Patient nationality and status.

Line 9: Contamination.

While I have assessed that Tony is stable, I do not have the luxury of a CT scan, and I would never assume that something far more sinister isn't going on. An X-ray computed tomography, or CT scan, is a medical imaging method employing tomography to create a three-dimensional image of the inside of an object; in medical usage, images of internal organs. In simpler terms, the CT is a body scanner that looks for abnormalities or potential bleeds that aren't showing on the outside.

The trouble with treating physically fit soldiers is that they can often disguise severe injuries until it's too late. Their fit bodies will sometimes mislead medics into thinking that all is well. The human body is an amazing piece of engineering: it's designed to shut down and protect itself. It will fool an untrained eye before free-falling at a rapid rate. I remember my time in Sierra Leone, when a British army officer walked away from a helicopter that had crash-landed. She died minutes later from a massive internal bleed. On the ground, we treat for the worst and hope for the best.

A close encounter with an RPG does not leave a healthy outcome in anyone, so with an air of caution, I administer Tony 10 mg of morphine. Because it's intramuscular (IM), it could take up to thirty minutes to take effect.

An IM medication is given by needle into the muscle. This is as opposed to a medication that is given by a needle, for example, into the skin (intradermal [ID]), just below the skin (subcutaneous [SC]), or into a vein (intravenous [IV]). Medics are issued morphine auto jets, each holding a one-hit IM dose of 10 mg. The method works when time is limited. I have never been a fan of this system; it's easier to monitor a patient's progress if the morphine is given intravenously. It can be titrated (diluted), and, therefore, faster acting and with less likelihood of overdose. In my view, this process can be very helpful. For example, in 2006, surgeons in Camp Bastion had to deal with an opiate overdose before getting stuck into the actual wounds. My theory on the administration of morphine is that a tiny amount of pain lets a casualty know that he is still alive; better still, it lets me know that he is alive.

I can manage a casualty easily if he is still with it. If the security situation deteriorates, his treatment will stop until our safety is re-established. Titration of morphine is the way forward, and most forward-operating medics like this system, along with the use of other pain-relieving drugs. Many of the grunts (infantry soldiers) on the ground often refuse morphine. No one wants to lie helplessly in such a hostile environment.

Without warning, Tony now starts to act erratically. *Did I misjudge the severity of his head injury?* For a second, I question myself. My own pulse increases, and my palms are suddenly sweaty. Shining my torch, I look deep into Tony's eyes, and then I reassess the wound. I check behind his ears and look up his nose, searching for anything that I may have missed. Any abnormal posture or seizures?

My panic is short-lived as Scotty McFadden comes in, telling Tony, 'Man up, ya fucker, and stop acting like a fuckin' lunatic.'

Tony starts to laugh. Using the buddy system to identify any type of traumatic brain injury is a great tool. Guys know their own soldiers, and Tony's behaviour wasn't at all out of character. Relief for me, and a morale boost for the troops watching the theatrics unfold.

Adding to all this, Abbie and Sean come bounding into the CAP with three additional casualties. All have multiple shrapnel wounds; one in particular requires urgent surgery to a wound penetrating his abdomen. We have a potential mass-casualty scenario, and Kev quickly updates the nine-liner.

Within twenty minutes, all casualties are stabilised. As my team finish off preparing our injured for evacuation, I disappear into the ops room to update the boss and get a 'wheels up' time from Kev. Wheels up is the time that the helo (or rescue bird) will leave Camp Bastion. This allows me, together with my team, the time we need to manoeuvre our injured out to the HLZ.

The attack came at last light, an age-old tactic adopted by every fighting force since the very barbaric yet successful days of both Genghis Khan in the East and the Romans in the West. The Taliban are creatures of habit, and generally attack from positions that have been successfully used before; this was employed time and time again to systematically slaughter the Russian occupiers during the late 1970s early '80s. It ensures that the attack is on the Taliban's terms and at a time of their choosing. They also know the area and all potential escape routes, including ours. In military terms, it's all about controlling the battle space – another piece of information I picked up during my time on the medical desk.

In 2006, our government believed that we could control Helmand with fewer than 4,000 troops. We sent 40,000 to Iraq, and by 2008, we had around 8,000 soldiers in southern Afghanistan – the most dangerous place on the planet. I didn't need a PhD to understand that our politicians may have underestimated just how many jihadists we were taking on.

News from Camp Bastion says that wheels are up; we have what is known as the 'golden hour' – a window of time in which to get casualties off the ground and into surgery as quickly as possible. Including our own treatment, the evacuation will be complete in just under an hour, including flight time. This is reassuring, and it offers our casualties the best possible chance of survival; hearing that the medical emergency response team (MERT) helicopter is airborne is welcome news. The MERT offers our casualties a secondary lifeline should they deteriorate on the rescue bird. The MERT are the unsung heroes of the battle to secure Helmand. The team is made up of highly qualified medical personnel who are capable of giving in-flight lifesaving treatment if and when required.

Sgt Maj. Davey Robertson leads a patrol from our base to secure the route to and from the HLZ. The chosen site is an old football pitch opposite our base on the other side of the canal. All of this is happening under the cover of darkness, and the young Jocks rely heavily on the basic low-level soldiering skills, which cover movement at night. With technology ever moving forward, it is sometimes easy to forget the basics. My team and I are on foot and carrying four extremely heavy casualties. Davey relays via a runner, confirming that the landing site is secure. My extraction group is ready, and we prepare to move.

The evacuation must be measured at all times with clear command and control. My role ends only when our casualties are airborne; until that time, I must keep a grip on the situation. Hearing the sound of the Chinook in the distance, my mind is buzzing with questions as I mentally check that I have covered everything. Which way is it going to land? Are we at the right end of the football pitch? Are my casualties stable enough? Who am I going to hand over to? My list is endless, and no one can answer the questions. My heart races again, and my palms are still sweaty.

The Chinook comes in low and fast, touching down amidst a huge cloud of debris. On the ground, the cool night air on my face is quickly warmed by the downdraught of the powerful double engines to the rear of the aircraft.

A small green light in the back allows me to identify the loadmaster, and also gives me a path to follow with my casualties. I give the handover notes to whoever is available, and then count off all of my team before giving a thumbs up to the door gunner. It was painless and went perfectly, just as we like it.

As the Chinook takes off, my team take cover. The downdraught almost blows me over. *Good positioning, Taylor,* I think to myself, replaying the landing in my head.

We double back to the safety of the PB. All command elements gather in the ops room for hasty orders. No surprise to find out that B Company and its support are staying in Nad-e Ali for the foreseeable future. The unstable tactical situation here has become a major cause for concern; with so few boots on the ground, we will struggle to provide total security. I expect more soldiers will be inbound, bringing with them supplies and equipment. All we can do as a company minus is kill as many Taliban as we can in an attempt to cripple the enemy's grip on the area. Isolated and very much alone, this could turn into a sizeable undertaking for the troops around me. As medics, we will of course support them as best we can.

Maj. Clark is concerned about Tony's condition, and Lt Col Nazim, the Afghan commander, is worried about his men. I reassure them both that I didn't envisage any major problems; however, any number of complications could occur. The balance of survivability is definitely in our favour; all we can do is wait for news from Camp Bastion. Another long day culminating in a casualty evacuation (casevac) has left every man exhausted.

Scanning our medical room and thinking about the questions that I often have that are never answered, I notice the silent, wide-eyed, panic-stricken faces. I am probably wearing the same expression myself. How were people reacting to combat stress and fatigue? In just forty-eight hours, so much already happened. The base was unsafe, and the blokes had yet to patrol out of it. I realise then that these men will come to rely heavily on me and my team; all of us in B Company know our roles tonight.

I need a decent night's sleep, but not before cleaning up the mess left behind by our injured. One thing is for sure: we haven't seen the last of spilt blood. Creatures of habit, we always square away our medical room, preparing to receive again at any time. Sorting through used bandages, my attention is diverted to something else, I overhear a conversation between the boss and the kandak commander. It seems like a heated argument, as both of them speak in slightly raised voices.

As I listen, I learn that the direct hit from the RPG has come from inside the base. An Afghan soldier fired low from the roof. Tony was manning the outer wall when he was struck by the RPG round.

The Jocks don't welcome this information at all. It's not the best start to relations between the two sets of soldiers. Amazingly, the grunts take the news in their usual relaxed and politically correct stride. Cries of 'cunts!' echo around the PB for the rest of the evening. Too tired to care, I laugh quietly at the absolute outrage of it all.

When all is said and done, the young Jocks realise that we have to fight alongside the Afghans if we are to stand any chance of surviving down here. The Afghan fighters are as knowledgeable as the Taliban when it comes to knowing the ground and terrain; their input is priceless, and it is our job to mentor them and introduce them to battle discipline. They have a medical team just like we do, and I am happy to mentor and guide them.

My throat is parched, and I down two bottles of water one straight after the other. I need sleep, and look down with less-than-eager eyes at my thin roll mat and my even thinner bivvy bag. A quick brush of teeth, and I lay my head for the night. Thinking about what will become of us, I still hold on to a glimmer of hope that we may return to Lashkar Gah.

In addition to being the capital of Helmand Province, Lashkar Gah is the seat of the provincial Afghan government. The base, in the centre of a heavily populated area, is home to the UK task force commander. I flew into Lash on a Chinook when I arrived twelve weeks ago, after initially landing in Kandahar aboard a Tristar.

I had been here briefly in 2006; many changes had occurred since then. The deployment of UK military forces in Lashkar Gah (LKG) followed a tradition for the area. LKG means 'army barracks' in Persian. LKG was established a thousand years ago as a riverside town for soldiers accompanying the Ghaznavid nobility to their seasonal winter capital of Bost. The ruins of the Ghaznavid manors still stand along the banks of the Helmand River.

The city of Bost and its outlying communities were mostly destroyed by the Ghorids, Genghis Khan, and Timur Lenk. Today the community of Bost is home to a hospital and airport. It also provides a great backdrop for photo opportunities to the increasingly popular military tourist. Steeped in history, the stunning scenery and Old World imagery provide a spectacular backdrop for photographic souvenirs.

Back in Nad-e Ali, at the old school, we as a company group are writing modern history. The thick walls offer more warmth than that of the roof from last night. Sleeping for what seems like five minutes, I soon imagine someone pressing the fast forward button on a really old video player. The glow of the morning sun is already upon me. A voice mutters excitedly, 'I have just managed four hours sleep!' I groan; it is not my voice. Grumbling and puffy-eyed, I look at the dirty grey ceiling of our CP and then gaze around the room, noting that everyone has that 'don't talk to me just yet' look about them.

B Company stands to as the sun rises over Nad-e Ali. In normal circumstances, this would be my favourite time of day. The sky is serene and beautiful, softening the sometimes harsh landscape. The sounds of the muezzin bring to an end our stand-to. The muezzin, a man appointed to call to prayer, climbs the minaret of the mosque and calls in all directions. Many mosques no longer require the muezzin to climb the minaret. Instead, a loudspeaker carries the message.

The mundane but necessary chores of morning routine are a welcome break from taking cover. My bladder feels like it is about to explode, and I can't recall the last time that I emptied it. Stumbling outside, I search the nearby vehicles for my multipurpose yellow sharps container. This small piece of kit is designed to hold discarded needles, syringes, and so forth (i.e., 'sharps'), but now it is affording me the luxury of a portable latrine. I have been using the handy piece of gear in this capacity for the last four months. Climbing into the back of a vehicle, I keep my dignity by balancing over the sharps container, out of sight of the base.

Stuck in what now feels like a stress position for an absolute eternity, thighs burning, I can't seem to finish. Moments like this make me wish that I had joined the Royal Air Force (RAF). Laughing for a second at my efforts, I try to stand up, succeeding eventually. Sleeping rough has left me with a few minor aches and pains. Smashing my head on the roof of the vehicle as I manoeuvre myself around sets me up for an awesome start to the day. Even the cumbersome Mark 6 Alpha helmet I'm wearing doesn't stop the vibrations from going straight to my skull. I need to wash my hands, but water is scarce. I pull a packet of wet wipes out of the map pocket in my trousers, take out a wipe, and clean away the grime and remnants of what looks like blood from my lower arms. Hunched over in the back of the wagon, I pull up my trousers. Taking a small clear bag from the top of my basic wash kit, I use it as a makeshift rubbish bin. These very basic things make life bearable in a place like Nad-e Ali.

If your personal administration is poor, you will not survive for very long in these conditions. My time teaching recruits all about basic field admin always reminded me how to deal with myself. After two years of showing them how to do it, I found this part easy: lack of sleep and self-imposed pressure would become my biggest challenges. My final chore is to brush my teeth; while I have no concerns about the rest of my body, furry teeth might stop me from functioning. It all comes down to personal choice, and my morale is instantly lifted when I have clean hands and teeth.

Stomach rumbling, I remember that I haven't eaten for a fair few hours now. My stained, grubby combats have become a little baggier around the waist – happy days! I dig out my rations from my day sack and start to sift through the culinary delights that I will be enjoying today. British army rations are for sustainability only; they aren't known for their Michelin star-rated menus. Perhaps I am being a bit harsh, but I would give my left arm for an American military ration pack right now, or 'meals ready to eat' (MREs), as they call them. A packet of M&Ms, lemon pound cake, chicken breast, and a mini bottle of Tabasco sauce can hide a multitude of tastelessness. Not today, though: corned beef hash and beans for breakfast. Starting my day like this is clever, as things will only ever improve!

It's not long before command elements are summoned to the ops room for routine orders. This becomes a regular event, regardless of the time of day or night. A PB can't just maintain itself. The boss needs to be confident that everyone in his team understands what is expected of them. B Company will send out our first patrol later today: Scotty McFadden will lead his platoon out to meet a combat logistic patrol (CLP) coming from Lash with a resupp.

As soon as the word *resupply* ('resupp' for short) is mentioned, I know that we are going to become very familiar with this morning's call to prayer. I'm grateful to have packed some basic reading material, albeit a pocket-sized medical manual. The main operating base (MOB) in Lash will be a ghost town with the majority of its force protection down here in Nad-e Ali. What's strange is that I am not as disappointed as perhaps I should be. In some crazy warped way, I hoped that we would revisit the badlands of Marjah, which lies south of Nad-e Ali. Kev and I often joked about the 'Battle for Marjah', having already felt the buzz of adrenaline that comes with close-quarter engagement.

The mixture of fear and excitement left us naively wanting a little more. As it goes, a new story was emerging: 'The Battle for Nad-e Ali'. This is what I thought I had signed up for; the word *combat* in my job title had finally come to fruition, and I didn't want to be back in Lash listening to someone else's war stories. Nad-e Ali had a different atmosphere than Lash; it was raw, feral countryside surrounded by the Taliban. I feel excited, nervous, tired, and scared, all at the same time. Above all, this is an experience that I have started to enjoy in a strange, almost macabre way. Wondering why I am drawn to such an unstable situation, I look at the blokes around me, realising that we all feel the same way. The fear we feel is healthy; it isn't the same as a fear of heights or any other phobia. This is fear that needs a reaction, and that reaction brings out the very best in people – well, so far, anyway.

The last forty-eight hours have given us a glimpse of what is yet to be thrown our way. The men in Scotty's platoon (we call it a multiple) start preparing themselves and their vehicles for the upcoming patrol. They will leave under the cover of darkness. I assign Jen Young to accompany them; she has spent the last four months with these guys, and they trust her implicitly. Abbie, Sean, and I set about establishing a bona fide CAP next door to the main CP, as this will make passage of information easy. I start preparing a wish list to send across the radio net back to HQ, and, going by the casualties that we have taken so far, I order above and beyond what would normally be required.

As lead medic with no doctor here, my responsibilities

include the provision of a mass-casualty and evacuation plan. Patients must be categorised correctly at all times; this plan will ensure that the distribution of medical assets at brigade HQ level happens efficiently and without unnecessary delay.

My secondary task on the PB is to assess environmental health issues; it's not glamorous, but it's a fundamental part of camp set-up and routine. Firstly I head to the toilet block that has been allocated to B Company; I get within five metres of the mud-brick walls and start to dry-heave on account of the smell. It appears that the Afghans prefer to use the outside walls as opposed to the block designed specifically as a toilet block! (I hoped the stench that greeted our arrival was a one-time thing, but no such luck.)

The toilet-block structure comprises of five single cubicles, each containing a single hole into the ground below. On the back wall of each cubicle, there is a head-height window looking straight over the perimeter wall and out into Taliban country – just like a murder hole. Already I imagine the scene of getting shot in the face while squatting over the hole.

'Hey, Channy, fancy getting shot in there, and one of us has to come and get you out?' one of the blokes says.

I acknowledge his banter by pointing out that they are the lucky ones sleeping next to the toilet block.

Making my way back to the ops room, I report my findings to Sgt Maj. Davey Robertson; between us, we take on the responsibilities of camp routine and security. After one trip to the toilet, Davey manages to acquire an old wooden chair. Removing the leather top, he makes a temporary toilet seat.

The day seems to go by in a flash, and with most jobs complete, the base is yet again plunged into twilight as last light looms. Stand-to orders are given. Like clockwork, the rounds start flying; this time, the Taliban concentrate their efforts on our gun positions, our best defence, much to their detriment.

Medi, the Afghan soldier who fired the RPG at Tony last night, waits patiently to redeem himself. With no target acquired, he is stood down from any type of RPG action, much to the relief of the junior Jocks manning the wall. The attack isn't sustained, and there are no casualties to report. All of Scotty's platoon mount up under the command of 2Lt Alexander Barclay. After waving them off, I take the time to relax in the medical room. Davey and Monty discuss possible options for Nad-e Ali, as well as who might be sent to support B Company.

Eating some biscuits fruit from my rations, I opt for lying out on one of the stretchers. I join in the discussion. 'Which medic do you want to come and get you if you get shot in the toilet block?'

An overwhelming majority announces, 'Sean will come and get us, and you can see us back in here.'

Our idle chat is interrupted as the radio net becomes busy. Listening intently to the traffic coming from next door, we hear that Scotty's multiple has touched base with the CLP: they are exchanging kit and equipment along with personnel. Our company 2IC is inbound, and he will assume his position when he gets in. Kev relays all information to the boss without exception.

The constant fear of an IED strike is never far away. The Taliban plant them at will, through the night, and, one way or the other, we find them – the following day or maybe a week from now.

Hoping for a day without a significant event in Nad-e Ali is at best never going to happen. Within minutes of moving off, the convoy is in serious trouble. A desperate-sounding voice is heard over the net.

'Hello, topaz zero alpha, this is topaz two zero. Vehicle down. Say again, vehicle down.'

The net is frantic, and the mood in the ops room suddenly changes. Maj. Clark is desperate for information, as the gravity of the situation on the ground is yet to be established.

'No contact report? What the fuck is going on out there?' he asks Kev.

Kev springs into action as I look on. 'Hello, topaz two zero, this is topaz zero alpha. Send sitrep (situation report). Over.' He starts to repeat the message. 'Hello, topaz two zero this is—' Before Kev can finish, the stricken call sign answers up.

'Topaz zero alpha, this is topaz two zero. We have one disabled vehicle that has rolled into the canal. Roger so far? Over.'

'Topaz zero alpha, roger.'

'Topaz two zero, there are multiple pax (personnel) trapped inside, and the canal is waterlogged. We have set up a security cordon and a rescue team on site of the vehicle. Over.'

'Topaz two zero, this is topaz zero alpha. Keep me updated, and let me know if you need us to deploy QRF, send LOCSTAT. Over.' (QRF is short for quick reaction force. LOCSTAT, in short, is location with grid reference.)

'Topaz two zero, roger that. Out.'

'Fuck me,' says Monty, adding, 'this is all we need.' He goes to warn the QRF, just in case they need to push out. It's dark, and the stricken call sign is in a precarious situation.

We all understand that it's not just the water that poses a threat; our guys are now firm in a position on the ground. The Taliban attack when you are most vulnerable, so Scotty's crew must act fast. I start to worry about our guys potentially drowning out there. Our vehicles, especially the snatch with its stupid box body, will prove difficult to extract from. The thought of being trapped in one as it fills with water doesn't conjure up a great picture. Drowning being right up there on my list of how not to die, regardless of people saying that it's peaceful after the initial struggle; unfortunately, it's the struggle that you are actually awake for.

The ops room waits for news, and it's not long before we are updated again. 'Hello, topaz zero alpha, this is topaz two zero. All pax have been extracted from the vehicle, which is now immobilised. Seeking permission to deny the stricken vehicle. Over.'

'Acknowledged your last... wait out.'

Getting permission to deny a vehicle – in other words to permanently disable it – must go through the chain of command back at brigade HQ.

With no means of bringing the stricken vehicle back in, the established procedure is to destroy it with high explosives and make sure that any sensitive equipment does not fall into enemy hands. All the while we wait, we have injured soldiers on the ground, pinned down to one location. Needless to say, B Company is in for another long evening.

Getting permission for a vehicle denial from brigade HQ is never easy. A logistician at HQ demands that our chain of command must exhaust all avenues before using high explosives. The boss loses patience.

Getting on to the net himself, Maj. Clark speaks to brigade HQ directly, advising, 'All avenues have been exhausted, and this is an extremely hostile AO (area of operation). Permission for the denial is required immediately. Over.'

There is a long pause. Everyone in the ops room is desperate for the right outcome. In less than a minute, HQ is back on the net: permission is granted. We all breathe a collective sigh of relief.

Maj. Clark's decisiveness has saved the day yet again, his tone on the net demanding the answer that he eventually gets. This situation has perfectly illustrated the reason why a person becomes an infantry company commander. Our OC's confident manner reassures us all that we are in more-than-capable hands.

The vehicle denial accomplished, our troubled convoy is moving again, finally limping into the PB well past midnight. Our medical team set about assessing our unexpected casualties. This time there is no blood or gore to patch up, only potential spinal problems and possible fractures.

With no life- or limb-threatening injuries, I advise the boss, 'Sir, a casualty lift at first light is possible, and no MERT is required straight away.' This affords Maj. Clark some time, as I further explain that these men are no longer capable of fighting.

The boss will always have the final say in the casevac of his men, as sometimes good medicine can mean bad tactics. The tactical situation must always have first consideration; extracting casualties in the middle of a firefight will potentially almost always create more casualties. It's a hard pill to swallow, but the best for the group is not always best for the individual. Our pilots will fly into anything – again, the line between brave and stupid has yet to be defined by soldiers, and that's the way we like it. A bureaucratic train of thought is best left in the office; on a PB, everyone must remain flexible, as plans may change in an instant.

Keeping all this in mind, just as I always do, I continue my current report to Maj. Clark, ever mindful that when I advise the boss in such instances, I do so as his subject matter expert (SME). As OC, it is his responsibility to weigh the pros and cons, and then to make the decision. I have learnt to always consider the tactical situation before coming to my own conclusion about casevac. Maj. Clark knows that I do this, and it reassures him.

'Sgt T,' he says now, 'we will evacuate the guys at first light. Have your team ready.'

'Roger, sir. Thanks.'

Once again, I feel that I am exactly where I'm meant to be, doing exactly what I'm meant to do. I used to get frustrated when soldiers from other armies asked why I opted to volunteer for tactical courses as a medic. When I qualified as an instructor in urban operational warfare in late 2007, it wasn't so that I could count up the hundred or so bruises I'd sustained, nor was it to marvel at the strange looks I would receive from the men of the Jordanian military with whom I found myself working alongside. I didn't go through that training just to teach other medics how to clear houses or villages. I did it to get a better understanding of potential casualty choke points, learning how an infantry company operates in a built-up urban area. I knew that the days of conventional warfare were over, and I welcomed any tactical course that would enable me to understand the ramifications of the decisions that I made on the ground. The courses were far from easy; however, there were always those who struggled with the very basics of soldiering far more than I did. This was an area I revelled in, and whenever it was my turn to carry the machine gun to give fire support, I ensured that I never wavered. I still do. Those courses were time well spent.

Using everything that I learnt, I now advise my peers and junior medics on how to best use difficult built-up terrain to evacuate casualties, and, more importantly, on how not to become a burden on the infantry company we supported. This includes everything we do – from MARCH-P to casevac, to maintaining supplies, and so on. That last thought brings me back to the wish list that I had begun to write earlier in the day. There's talk of a helicopter resupp, so I get my head around what we will need if our casualty rate continues at the current pace.

I finish the wish list, eventually hitting my roll mat in my pit space well past two in the morning. My team and I are out on the ground tomorrow, so we need rest. And yet, seemingly within seconds of closing my eyes, I hear the dreaded shout of 'Stand to!'

'What the fuck!' I groan as I get eyes on Kev. I must have slept soundly; it just never feels like enough. With no snooze button to press, like a robot I get up, put on my body armour, and secure the chinstrap on my helmet.

Making my way into the medical room, I find the rest of my team. Good to see that everyone else looks the way that I feel: like crap. Same detail as yesterday. Stand-to is called at times of attack or times of habitual enemy attack; first and last light are favoured, so we get up and take positions that have been allocated to us by the chain of command. I gather my med team, and we wait for a period of time before being given the order to stand down. It's a routine that's adopted by every fighting force the world over, with some more disciplined than others, I imagine.

Call to prayer is my call to the yellow multipurpose sharps container. Climbing into the back of the snatch Land Rover, I think about the non-politically-correct army poster that read: 'No one likes a dirty snatch.' Of all the things to think of, this lifts my mood as I go about my personal chores.

News from the ops room says that wheels will be up from Camp Bastion shortly, so my team begin to tend the wounded. We have four sorry-looking soldiers, and a night in the cold has not helped their now-rigid bodies. Mild whiplash will feel like a broken neck this morning. We have no means of spinal control, and, as they do with everything else, grunts crack on unless they are physically unable to do so. Making the best use of the equipment that we have, we walk our wounded.

One stretcher is out under the watchful eyes of Sgt Maj. Robertson's team, who have already secured the routes in and out to the HLZ.

The helicopter, a Sea King, lands and is on the ground no longer than twenty seconds. As it rises, it creates a spiral of dust. This time, I have positioned myself so that I don't get blasted by the debris from the ground.

Again running back to the PB, I see preparations for a foot patrol are under way. Sean will deploy out this morning. Jen is getting some well-earned rest after her late night. Abbie and I settle in to the ops room, on standby should we be required to deploy out with the QRF.

Daydreaming about what day it is, I doze off in a sweaty pool on my roll mat. Abbie wakes me on account of my snoring. I would normally be a little embarrassed, but in this arena I couldn't care less. Counting six hours sleep in the last three days, and in a stimulant-free state, I am running on empty. I feel myself getting agitated – my head feels fuzzy, and little things are starting to irritate me. Moving next door to the medical post to chat with Davey gives me a decent escape, but it isn't long before I am sprawled out on the stretcher, snoring again.

Three hours later, Davey wakes me up, laughing.

'We have just taken a wee bit of small arms, Channy,' he says.

I managed to sleep through the attack. Feeling refreshed again, I get the brews on. Rest is a major part of routine, and sometimes, with all chores covered, you take it when and where you can.

CHAPTER 3

THE SHOOTING SEASON

INTELLIGENCE REPORTS FROM HQ REVEAL THAT MORE Taliban fighters are heading for Nad-e Ali from across southern Helmand; insurgent activity on the ground has increased significantly. The fresh jihadists coming from the south are happily battling it out with our neighbours, A Company of 5 Scots, who hold the line down in Garmsir. If the fighters survive Garmsir, they skirt around Marjah, stopping only for replenishment of food, water, and ammunition before hitting us.

Nad-e Ali sits extremely close to Lashkar Gah. Defeat here would be a strategic disaster. The so-called shooting season has reached its pinnacle. Our PB is isolated; it's easy to feel that brigade HQ has forgotten about us.

The threat of one of our helicopters being shot down is now so high that aircraft will only fly in to our PB at night or at dawn. Once on the ground, the pilots don't hang around; they drop off or pick up, and are airborne within seconds to reduce the chance of an attack. Tactical aviation planners try to make sure that the Chinooks don't establish patterns when flying. To any observer though, not creating a pattern indirectly creates one.

When helicopters come to the base, as explained, it is at night or first thing in the morning, thus creating a pattern.

Most of us in B Company have deduced that we are here for one reason: to make sure the Taliban don't mount any form of attack on the Kajaki operation. We aren't a company complete, and our casualty rate is unsustainable. The Kajaki mission has been on the cards for months. We all understand that it's the main focus of the 'big picture' for our brigade, but we know very little about the operation. As with most ops, soldiers on the ground are kept in the dark.

We know the basic aim of the Kajaki mission: the delivery of a third turbine, to get the hydro-electric dam to work at full capacity, providing power to Kandahar and southern Afghanistan. If successful, the operation will be the catalyst to kick-start future development. It will also make history as the coalition's biggest campaign in the south. The Taliban aren't a hearts-and-minds organisation. I don't believe that their fighters at the ground level really know what's going on, either; they are likely kept more in the dark than we are. Their 'big picture' could be very different from ours, and is possibly funded by individuals who have no interest in a 'better' Afghanistan.

Every commander likes to throw around the 'big picture'. Troops on the front line quickly grow to dislike these words. When you are stinking, piss-wrapped with sweat, walking around in seven-week-old pants, eating shit food, and constipated from that shit food, the last thing you want to hear is 'big picture'.

So, yes, the 'big picture' was starting to piss everyone off, including me. Soldiers understand that there is a task to complete, we take our orders, complete our missions, and leave it at that. Save the bullshit part of the mission for dinner parties. In general, troops on the ground want to know two things: (1)

when are we going home? and (2) when are our replacements arriving?

Time passes on the PB, and it soon comes to light that we are not alone here in Nad-e Ali as first thought. It's a relief to find a friendly call sign just about a kilometre away from our own location. The soldiers, special operations reservists, are housed in the old prison, just outside the district centre. Their role in Helmand is to train and mentor the Afghan police. They make up part of the police mentoring team (PMT).

The title PMT, with its potentially humorous connotation of pre-menstrual tension, raises a fair few smiles, so we decide to rename their unit's call sign, using a moniker of their own – 'the Throatcutters' – which sounds far more gnarly. I have no doubt that there will soon be a unit T-shirt available, with 'Throatcutters' emblazoned across the front. If not across the front of a T-shirt, maybe on the back of a North Face jacket? All kidding aside, these guys have been operating across Helmand for the last two months; living with the Afghans, their small outposts were smashed on a daily basis.

The happiness of discovering friendly neighbours close by is soon supplanted by our ongoing grim reality. Shock horror as our base comes under attack again, with the gun position on the roof doing most of the heat seeking. Scotty Pew and his men must be putting a sizeable dent in enemy numbers: the Taliban are desperate to take that gun position out. Thankfully, the sandbag-reinforced walls are doing a sterling job in holding the insurgents' high-velocity rounds at bay. The task of daily rebuilding this reinforcement is a dangerous, back-breaking effort for the lads; however, the benefits far outweigh the negatives. Pew works on a shift system for his men on the roof. The gun teams sleep up there, as movement up and down those steps leaves them wide open to enemy fire. The wall is riddled with holes from incoming 7.62mm.

We receive news that the Afghan police station where we spent our first night has been hit hard: initial reports over the net confirm three casualties. The Afghans are instructed to bring their wounded to our location. Their main compound has taken a couple of direct hits from RPGs. We were there just nights ago; I am beginning to think that Lady Luck plays a big part in all of this. Skill alone doesn't decide who lives or who dies. Time and place both play a huge part in what happens on the battlefield. Many serving in the military adopt the attitude that if it's your time, it's your time – you could be the best soldier in the world, but a stray round or indirect fire (IDF) might just have your name on it. It's not a pleasant thought, but how else could we do what we do?

These are passing thoughts, and I quickly refocus. I have one medic out on the ground, so there are three of us left, including me. We prepare our aid post for the incoming casualties, every man busy.

I suddenly notice the smell coming from underneath my body armour. It's not good, but there's little water, so a decent scrub is almost impossible. Most soldiers don't mind their own smell. There is definitely a time and a place for girl stuff; I do that when I go home, leaving the baggy, earth-tone clothing in Afghanistan and going back to being normal for a bit.

I can't imagine anything worse than worrying about trying to look attractive out here. I have never had the patience for it. Thinking of it now, I recall an incident during pre-deployment training when I watched in horror as a scenario based on the 'escalation' drill unfolded. A female soldier who was deploying to Camp Bastion as a post/mail orderly (not from my unit I hasten to add) could not engage a target because her fingernails were too long! Taking the incident in my normal relaxed stride, I said, *What the fuck are you smoking?* I was outraged with the usual weak-minded guys around me who seemed to think that it was okay because she was just in charge of the mail. It's not okay, and it never will be.

The thoughts about body odour and fingernails flash out of my mind as quickly as they flashed in. We wait patiently for the ANP casualties to turn up. When they arrive, they're ferried straight in. Yet again, they aren't too concerned that they are receiving treatment from female soldiers. Initial eyes on give indications of one cat-B and two cat-Cs. There are lots of fragmentation wounds to limbs, which is no surprise. On average, a soldier in any type of blast will usually present with over nine injuries, and not all will be catastrophic. Usually the ones not seen are the danger; if I can see it, I can fix it – or at least try to.

As a female soldier, I recognised early on that medicine is possibly the only way in which a woman can get away with interacting with the men of this culture, specifically in this country. Males run these societies, and women are regarded as second-class citizens. I have many friends in a variety of cultures, and I struggle to understand some of their traditions as much as I expect they do mine, but Afghanistan under the rule of the Taliban encourages systematic abuse, torture, and the absolute maltreatment of women. That is something that I neither accept nor comprehend, and I never will.

The injured men don't want to touch our hands, and we don't force our personal beliefs upon them. We accept the cultural differences, and as soldiers, our mission will always come before any personal gripe – this is why we fare so well. Medicine has broken down barriers the world over, and as yet, it is the only thing to do so. After a quick medical assessment, I leave Abbie and Sean to crack on, and go to initiate the nine-liner to HQ. It's a luxury to have such high-calibre medics in my team; they make my job seem easy at times.

Kev relays the nine-liner to brigade HQ, including all of the information that I have given him. He occasionally likes to add his own spin to messages, so Maj. Clark snaps at him to relay the information word for word.

'Cpl Coyle, if I relay something to you, I need it repeated word for word, is that clear?'

'Roger that, sir.' Kev looks at me with a naughty childlike grin.

The use of 'Cpl Coyle' and not 'Kev' tells him that he is in the shit.

No one is immune to getting gripped by the boss, and rightly so. If you have never been rebuked by your commander, you are definitely doing something wrong. Free thinking makes for a better fighting force, so long as that thinking is not *too* free.

I return to the medical room to check in on my guys. After quick medical interventions, the three casualties are stable enough for evacuation. The policemen have gotten off lightly; having said that, getting used to battle injuries has made me look at the body in a different light. Head injury? Very vascular area produces a lot of blood; could still be superficial. Abdominal injury? Looks nasty – anything perforated? No? Okay then – wrap, seal position, and move on. At times, injuries appear like a well-crafted training scenario.

Another crisis has been avoided; surely that is our lot today. Losing count of the casualties that we have treated, we make the now-familiar trip out to the HLZ. The Afghan soldiers on the base help to carry the stretchers onto the Chinook. They haven't been trained in any type of helicopter handling, so giving a lesson with real-time casualties has turned into a scene out of *Ren and Stimpy*. I have come to believe that if you see it in a cartoon, you will most definitely see it in Afghanistan – and, more than likely, it will be with Afghan soldiers. Our militaries are trained to a very high standard; we control all of our movement in any given scenario through the use of all of our senses. The Afghans don't, so two things can happen: either nothing or unorganised chaos, usually resulting in death or serious injury. They have no sense of danger at all, and on the battlefield, their 'bravery' is often out of all proportion to their sense of fear.

The current situation is by no means atypical. In 2006, when the first British troops arrived in the area men from the Royal Irish (RI) Regiment were assigned to mentor Afghan army units. After a fierce battle in Garmsir, the RI reported that the Afghans were not of sound mind, refusing to take cover in a contact and running straight towards the enemy. When their commander was shot dead, the soldiers stopped fighting and prepared to mourn his death. They had to be 'fired up' by RI soldiers to make sure they went back into battle. It dawns on me in the midst of the evac that Afghan tactical awareness is very different from that of UK forces. I take this evacuation slowly and use hand signals to direct the team, nice and simple and easy to understand.

We return to the medical room and quickly replenish the kit used. Once again, I retreat to the peace and quiet of my aid post to catch a couple of hours sleep. The noise from the radio next door ensures that it is never a deep one. It's not long before I learn that Scotty's boys are in trouble. I rouse quickly and head straight into the ops room. They are just over a kilometre away: their vehicle patrol is hit, and through the haze of battle, it emerges that one of the wagons is cut off. My heart is literally pushing at my throat at the thought of any of our lads being captured. The boss is beside himself.

Panicked voices over the radio net are not painting a good picture. Monty is already mounted up, ready to provide QRF to the stricken patrol. It's times like this when an experienced commander does not make a knee-jerk reaction. Monty is chomping at the bit to get to Scotty, but the boss knows that sending more troops to the ambush site will only add to our woes. Plus, it could have potentially disastrous consequences until we know exactly what's happening on the ground. This is the first time that I've really gotten to see the boss at work. Maj. Clark is pacing up and down, going through every possible scenario.

He speaks calmly and directly. 'Monty, stand your men to, and await further orders.'

'Roger that, sir,' Monty replies.

In one motion, he has eased Monty's tension by standing the QRF to. Monty will now go off and rally his men; in turn, they will prepare themselves mentally to help their mates. It's a psychological victory for all, and yet no one is moving anywhere. When you are on the outside of a situation looking in, you see why certain things are said or done. The last thing the boss needs is to send more troops to an already perilous situation; this would be a last resort for him. His soldiers need direction, and good commander that he is, that is exactly what he will give them.

Barclay is the young platoon commander in charge out on the ground. Barely out of Sandhurst Military Academy (British army officer training), 2Lt Barclay will be running through options of where the vehicle may have gone. Together, he and Scotty will make a quick combat estimate, finding a workable plan.

By now, the boss has eyes on the area with the use of a video link from an unmanned aerial vehicle (UAV) drone.

Barclay's estimate will be uncomplicated and direct. In his mind, he will calculate a question: So, what is happening? We are missing a vehicle and three of my men. Therefore, I need to go back into the kill zone to get them. His combat estimate is then complete. His platoon, his soldiers, do not question his decision for a second; they are just desperate to find their missing comrades.

The ops room is silent. We sit staring at each other for a few seconds before we go back to staring at the radio. Even if Barclay does find the guys, the Taliban may have gotten to them first. It doesn't take long to kill someone. During our pre-deployment training back in the UK, it was made clear to us that if the Taliban capture you, it is likely that you will be killed. They will execute you and possibly film it for distribution on the Internet.

Fifteen minutes pass, and still there is no news. It is becoming unbearable – everyone's worst nightmare. Barclay is still searching, but there is still no sign of the missing WMIK. Another fifteen minutes pass, and then sound bursts from the radio: 'Man down! Man down!'

Through our interpreters via ICOM chatter (this is the interception of enemy transmissions via interim communications operations method [ICOM]), we can hear Taliban commanders and their men closing in on our stricken vehicle. My heart races, and my palms are sweaty again. Silence follows. I know everyone is wondering the same thing I am: *What is going on out there?*

I start overthinking the situation, and I force myself to stop this speculative train of thought. Instead, I do well to concentrate on what's actually happening. More information is coming through, and, suddenly, relief – the boss's face says it all. They have found the missing soldiers, and every Jock manning the walls outside is desperate for the news. I am relieved but still anxious, eager to get hold of my wounded. Time is precious when soldiers are bleeding. The platoon eventually break contact, and the men head back to the base.

There are three casualties we prepare for a speedy evacuation. The platoon commander's driver, LCpl la Roux, has bilateral injuries to his ears. Blood oozes from both of them, and his balance is non-existent; this the result of a close encounter with an RPG. Scotty has multiple fractures to the small bones in his hand, and young Lt Barclay has a gunshot wound to his upper thigh. (Barclay would later receive the Military Cross for his actions.) Tonight's casualties mean three more out of the game; with men injured on a now-daily basis, something will have to give. The Afghan soldiers must be forced to stand and fight with B Company; if they don't, Nad-e Ali will fall.

Barclay and Scotty are reluctant to go; losing command elements of any unit is a bitter pill to swallow. Barclay is just starting out in his career. For him, this is what he has spent the last eighteen months training for. I remind him that he has been shot; between them, they saved the lives of three soldiers. Fear does funny things to the soul; words on a page cannot ever truly describe the gut-wrenching nausea that you feel when rounds are zipping by. The non-politically-correct term of 'my arse felt like it was about to fall out' is the only description that even comes close. It might be the result of the shift in fluid that takes place in the body during the onset of shock, or the flight-or-fight scenario that's a gift from the central nervous system.

Leaving no time to dwell on the incident, trouble magnet Duffy comes bounding in. 'A direct hit, Channy. Happy days, mucker!' He is describing his direct hit on the enemy closing in on the lads; eyes on, he engaged with a 66 mm grenade launcher. His action tipped the odds in our favour.

Cpl Gaz Wallace was the vehicle commander who was cut off with two others. As the night drifts on, I notice that Gaz is unusually quiet; I wonder if he's okay, as he took in and maybe pondered on what could have been. I will catch up with him if he needs me; a soldier sometimes needs a moment to put situations into perspective. I don't badger him; a friendly tap on the shoulder will do. We are a tight-knit group, and the lads know that our door is always open. The latest casevac results in another clean-up of our CAP.

Later in the evening, the banter starts to fly around the base, with taunts of what might have been if the guys were taken prisoner. Jokes about orange boiler suits and getting bummed by the Taliban are rife. With the Jocks, the insults are never far away, and they provide a good indicator that morale is still okay. In fact, the more inappropriate the better; this is the way that we all deal with the emotional trauma.

The news that more guys are heading our way is well received. We have already welcomed the PMT, and now a training unit called the OMLT (operational mentor and liaison team) are inbound. The OMLT is a small six-man training team; they will hopefully give direction to our Afghan brothers and help shape them. They have deployed from a much bigger UK training formation based near Camp Bastion. They don't have a medic, so I loan them one of ours. I choose Sean for the task, as it's a small team of six men working closely with the Afghans.

While the ANA accept our help medically in the base, I do not wish to push my luck by sending a female to live with and support them. Our numbers are falling fast, so the arrival of the OMLT will give us a much-needed uplift both in morale and numbers – six is better than zero.

Monty, now the sole platoon sergeant, faces a lot of responsibility. He has Cpl Jay Henderson as his second in command (2IC). Hendy from Wishaw is more than capable of holding the platoon together. Monty also has Davey and me on hand for support should he need it. Infantry soldiers are trained at least one up if needed; it's not uncommon for commanders to be killed or wounded on the battlefield.

Thankfully, Monty is a strong senior non-commissioned officer (SNCO) who looks older than his years; his men admire him, and my medics feel safe with him. He is a typical Scotsman: likes a drink and smokes as many cigarettes as the day will allow. He is also a soldier that I learn a great deal from.

Given my mum's background, I have no problems getting heavily involved in the Jock banter. Take young Ferris, for instance. 'Shut it, ya wee fanny' is a phrase that he often receives. Ferris is a comical young Jock who taunts all of the junior blokes and medics. Without realising it, he has become the soldiers' morale booster, and he is always looking for an opportunity to act up. If he is not waking one of the other grunts up with the vision of his rear end or private parts right next to their face he is seeking out soldiers at their lowest point, trying to get a snap out of someone. Once the snap is complete, you will find the soldier recently at his lowest now laughing away with the rest of the troops. 'Ferris therapy' would never be approved by a medical board, but it works. I knew Ferris when I was a depot instructor. He was a young recruit when our paths first crossed. It's hard to believe that we are now fighting alongside each other. He was the same then as he is now – a pest! I shake my head and laugh now, seeing his very white arse hanging out of a large hole in the back of his combats. This hole is from the wear and tear of the skirmishes that he has been in thus far, and he makes no attempt to cover it. It will no doubt soon provide a laugh for the other Jocks, if it hasn't already.

Settling down into my bed space, I dig out my iPod and engross myself in the solace of some of my favourite tunes. I select a top twenty-five from my library, knowing this playlist will see me through the rest of this tour. My iPod turns out to be my one saving grace during these testing times.

Lying in the dark between Jen and Abbie, I think about my brother David. He was killed in 2002 when I was on exercise in Cyprus. David was trying to defuse a situation in the street outside a casino when he was killed. He was a non-aggressive person, which made his death hard to cope with. I keep a small picture of him in the inner sleeve of my body armour. It's always there and very important to me. Along with the photo is a set of rosary beads. A friend of David's gave them to me to put in his casket. I didn't have the heart to tell her that his casket was already closed, so I kept them with me instead. I never thought of the beads as a religious symbol; they were simply full of memories of my brother.

A year after David was killed, I deployed to southern Iraq. Looking back, I don't think I went through a natural grieving process. My grief would not surface until much later. The photo and rosary beads saw me through some rough times during my tours of Iraq in 2003 and Helmand in 2006. They are still with me on this tour, so if they get me home safe, they will stay with me forever.

Losing David was the worst thing that ever happened to me; the thought of losing blokes tonight reminded me of him. I was sure that if I were to die out here, my one consolation would be that I would get to see David again. The month after his death, I sifted through every inch of medical paperwork that there was on his case file. I tortured myself day and night, endlessly reliving the incident. I was also searching for someone to blame; as a medic, I felt both angry and guilty that I had not been there to save him.

I do not have long to reflect on my feelings about David or anything else. In the next instant, I am up and running around in my body armour and helmet. The Taliban have let rip another onslaught. For a split second, I think that they must have known I was having a 'moment'. This momentary grim humour aside, the truth is that every attack is getting a little too close for comfort. Their IDF may not be as accurate as the Taliban would like, but we all know that it only takes one lucky shot for someone's day to end badly. Not today, though.

I always appreciate that every man out here has a story to tell, so I dust myself off and move on, safe in the knowledge that my brother will be watching over me from somewhere. I tally up the casualties, mentally noting who was injured, and when. My body and mind alike are fatigued. I gather the medical team and make sure that they are okay. I may be in a command position, but these are my guys, and their safety is always my concern. We would become great friends during our time in Nad-e Ali. My medics and I are involved with every attack, whether inside or outside of the base. We rely heavily on each other to get things right.

I think back to the summer 2006 when I deployed here with 3 PARA. I never fully understood what it meant to be under siege when the young paratroopers spoke about the battle for Sangin. Nad-e Ali was turning into our Sangin – you had to be in the shit to understand what it felt like.

The true lay of the land is known only by the enemy; this is their backyard, and they know every inch of it. When most units deploy into a base such as Nad-e Ali, they are supported by a small artillery unit, as well as an engineer squadron building up defensive walls. We have nothing: we were sent on patrol, and now we are holding a line that is very much closing in on us. The one useful asset that we managed to steal from the Throatcutters was a joint tactical air controller (JTAC), usually assigned to special ops. Remaining nameless and in the shadows, he saved more than a few lives, and for that we will always be grateful.

For the most part, things are grim and getting grimmer. Rations are quite literally being rationed. The young men fighting are ageing well beyond their years. Our intelligence support is superior on all levels, along with our interpreters, who give our company clear understanding of the Taliban's intentions and plans through ICOM chatter. It's evident that we are outnumbered: every village within a five-kilometre radius is housing Taliban fighters. Plans are afoot to overrun our small PB, but I wouldn't learn this little belter until months later.

Another night passes. Activity in the PB starts early; everyone is up as Monty prepares to take his platoon out. As soon as any patrol leaves, everyone goes on to a heightened state. The thought of being overrun is always at the forefront of my mind. One of our guys has already killed at least twenty fighters. He doesn't shout about it, but his success is well known across the company. The Apache gunships that have been regular visitors have torn up many more.

The Taliban's battlefield replacement plan seems to be working well: no matter how many we kill, they are able to replace them, and fast. We are lucky if we have two full platoons left. Monty's platoon is out for less than half an hour before getting hit. I can hear Monty's fire control orders clearly over the net; it's almost as if he is standing in the same room.

He calls for CAS, and our JTAC wastes no time in getting it to him. It sounds like some of the lads have been pinned down on the wrong side of a ditch. It's not like the films where you can run along tracks and dodge rounds. If you are up and running, the likelihood of getting shot generally multiplies.

Cpl Tam Rankine, one of the more-experienced section commanders, knows that the boys are in trouble. He sprints across the open ground to try to give them more fire support. During this rescue, he is shot in the hand, getting off lightly.

After more accurate use of the 66 mm, the men manage to make good the ground that they have lost. Jen treats Tam when she can, calling in her casualty over the net. The guys are in the middle of a firefight, so it's down to me and Sgt Maj. Robertson to go out to retrieve our wounded. My man Duffy has also been injured, and it doesn't surprise me that he is in the thick of it.

The Throatcutters are operating elsewhere, but they provide our QRF. We set off in three vehicles. I'm top cover for Davey, and there's a 66 mm rocket beside me. As I check the 66 mm, it dawns on me just how lucky I am – my path in life could have been very different. I am in a world that few men or women have the chance to experience. All medics that hail from 16 Brigade who are attached to infantry companies are given an insight into all the weapon systems that the company employs.

The Taliban attack any call sign, and when it heads south, everyone, regardless of job description or cap badge, can look forward to getting a slice. This is not a conventional conflict with prisoner of war (POW) camps. The Geneva Conventions actually means something in such conflicts, but it means nothing here. The waving of a Red Cross flag doesn't cut it, either. The soldiers that I support are fighting hard, and I would feel ashamed if I couldn't offer a safe haven to them when they are injured. As medics, we protect our casualties by any means necessary.

We head to where the fire is coming from; driving into contact is not for the faint-hearted. All I can think about is that hideous heavy weapon that the Taliban have been smashing the base with. A direct hit from the DShK would cut me in half. I look in the distance through the sight on top of my SA-80 (also called a SUSAT, for sight unit small arms trilux). I spot Jen running with her casualties. The noise is deafening. Davey also sees Jen, and he makes a hasty stop.

We get out of the vehicles and pick our blokes up. I watch Jen go running back to the platoon sergeants group. Together, she and Monty just crack on. I like the fact that you can't tell her apart from the others. When it's real time, soldiers are soldiers – the guys don't see Jen the female medic running towards them; they see 'our' medic.

The running we did around the HLZ back at Lash, always wearing our heavy body armour, is now paying off handsomely. I get my casualties in the wagon, and we head back to the PB. Once there, I examine Tam and Duffy. As per usual, Duffy finds something to joke about, laughing at the fact that they were 'shitting themselves when they were cut off.' I am relieved that Duffy is okay. Losing someone so young doesn't bear thinking about, and I have grown quite fond of his once-annoying habits.

The boss needs a casualty report, and fast. I assess a gunshot wound to the hand and possible fracture to the lower limb both as cat-Cs, which means we have four hours to play with. Distal pulses on both are good, so they should be okay. Thinking tactically, I know the firefight hasn't finished, so at the moment, the chance of more casualties is very high. Risking airframes for casualties that we can hold and treat is a non-starter. Sorting out fluids for both my injured, I think about the heat down here; it's stifling today. The platoon eventually breaks contact: the guys are heading back in. I discover that Kev has already sent a nine-liner declaring that we have a cat-B casualty. I am angered by the lack of communication. This has become commonplace on the battlefield, and sometimes medics are too scared to speak out.

This is the wrong decision, and so I approach Maj. Clark, my OC. I get on well with the boss and Kev, so I don't want any type of confrontation; nor do I want to make a situation out of nothing. Explaining to the major that the guys' injuries do not require such a high priority, I advise him that we should change the category back down to a C.

Maj. Clark acknowledges my point, but then says, 'What if the MERT team won't come because Tam is just a cat-C?'

I explain that there may be more needy casualties upcountry, and if we start overcategorising patients, brigade HQ will question all of our nine-liners. Anxious, I want the boss to agree with me. I understand what he is feeling, and his actions are always for the benefit of his men. I just want him to trust me, and know that I need his support on this. I further explain that I will send a casualty update over the net every fifteen minutes to ensure that they know four hours is our cut-off time – if we wait any longer than that, the damage to Tam's hand will become permanent. The MERT commander can review the downgrade to cat-C and then make an informed decision. The boss agrees and allows me to downgrade Tam and Duffy. No one is at fault here. Kev heard that Tam had a gunshot wound and automatically thought he was a cat-B. I am relieved that this has been resolved, and if anything, it has cemented my relationship with the boss. I set about preparing Tam and Duffy for evacuation.

The rest of Monty's platoon get back, and Davey meets them at the gate with water and rehydration sachets of Lucozade. This soon becomes a routine chore. Whoever has been out receives water and a Lucozade sachet at the front gate when they get back in. It's a good way to simultaneously check the morale and physical well-being of the men. Just looking at a soldier's face and body language can tell you a great deal. It's a far better system than allowing soldiers to quietly go off and administer themselves. If heat illness goes untreated, it becomes deadly very quickly.

A few of the lads come into the medical post to check on Duffy and Tam. We receive word that the MERT team and their Chinook are preparing to launch from Camp Bastion to pick up our casualties. This is welcome news. The boss and Capt. Wood, our company 2IC, both reassure me that we made the right call with Tam. I am relieved that the MERT team made the decision to come. We all put our faith in the system, and it has worked this time. Sometimes there may be a casualty far more desperate for the casevac than we are; other times it might be the reverse. I take a moment to think about my friends up north manning the FOBs. Our brigade is taking the fight to the Taliban at all levels, and in doing so, we sustain many casualties.

The MERT call prompts us to push ourselves out towards the front gate. We get our casualties in the shade, and then we sit and wait. I contemplate taking them back up to the aid post, as I am informed that the MERT helicopter has yet to launch. I check in with Kev at the ops room, and he tells me that the helicopter is finally wheels up at Camp Bastion, so it is on its way.

A few of the lads have joined our group to bid farewell to their muckers. I see that Stevie Howie is in the group. Stevie is a tough lad brought up on a rough council scheme in Glasgow. He has a strong character and manages to look as fresh as a daisy, even though he has just endured a two-hour contact during the hottest part of the day.

Without warning, there is a feeling of panic and danger around us. An Afghan soldier narrowly misses me and my casualties with his Ford Ranger pickup truck. 'Jesus fuckin' Christ!' someone screams. The driver isn't even a metre away; we are inches from his wheels. The idiot doesn't even see what he has done; he just continues to drive on, leaving us in a heap on the ground.

Stevie jumps up, going berserk. He brings his weapon to bear at the Afghan and starts yelling, 'You stupit fuckin' prick! You stupit fuckin' prick!'

Everyone in the group adds their ten-pence worth. Our guys are taking the brunt of the casualties out on the ground, and this wanker nearly mows down about six of us in the PB. The Afghan soldiers have been refusing to go out of the base, so this heightens an already tense situation. We manage to calm Stevie down, and I am relieved to hear the sound of a Chinook in the distance. I tell the guys that we need to push out. Stevie showed tremendous restraint at not losing it completely. It would be naive to judge his actions; he just spent the last two hours fighting off the Taliban, only to meet this threat inside the wire.

Duffy places his arm around my neck and shoulders as I help him hobble onto the ramp of the Chinook. Abbie does the same for Tam. As quick as the wheels are down, they are off again. I receive a reassuring pat on the back from the door gunner on my way off. It catches me off guard, and I wonder if he knows something that I don't.

Abbie turns and says, 'I guess that we are here for the long haul then, or at least until the marines take over.'

Great news, I think. That is just shy of two months away!

I run back to base and seek out Maj. Clark to explain the truck incident, making sure he knows all the facts before the situation gets out of control. He heads off for an informal chat with Lt Col Nazim. The ANA soldiers need much guidance with reference to discipline. We can't risk a blue-on-blue situation, so the arrival of the OMLT can't come quick enough.

Mundane tasks are completed again before anyone relaxes. Water is guzzled by the gallon on every corner after another event-filled day. Watching the sun go down over Nad-e Ali is a welcome display of serenity; the quiet hum of the guys' voices chatting offers a measure of peace in the midst of what is becoming a desperate time for B Company of 5 Scots.

CHAPTER 4

FLASHHEART ARRIVES

THE BASE SETTLES DOWN AS WE WAIT FOR OUR USUAL twilight attack. It arrives like clockwork: the initial strikes come from a variety of small arms; the follow-up of random bursts from .50 calibres and the throaty DShK are a timely reminder that the Taliban are equipped with more than just their ability to lay IEDs. What they lack in skill and discipline they make up for with their will to keep going. When you choose to take on an insurgency brainwashed and under the influence of the opium poppy, you should not find it surprising that they never tire of being killed. Pausing for a second in the midst of it all, I think about how bad life must be for a person to feel that way. But this is how it is with the Taliban. As soon as one fighter falls, another is on hand to pick up his AK-47. I have seen the exchange on the battlefield, bodies dragged away so quickly, you would miss it if you blinked.

Our group cracks on, optimism filling the air. Banter and insults start flying around, so the blokes' spirits must be as high as they were on day 1. The mocking moves to my music, which is taking its share of incoming. The Counting Crows play through a small speaker that I have stashed in my day sack. Certain items make life bearable in times of strife, so along with my yellow sharps container, the speaker is a must for my sanity. I mentally run through the music that has seen me through various combat tours.

In 1999, during operations in Kosovo, I was sent to a platoon recce house which overlooked the border with Serbia. Van Morrison was played to death in the house. Intelligence reports concentrated on threats of incursion, along with potential kidnapping. We filled our limited downtime with card games, and the essential light discipline likened our rooms to small, illegal gambling dens. The shadow of toe-tapping to 'The Bright Side of the Road' was my only visual during those experiences.

Paul Simon's *Graceland* provided the background music for Sierra Leone in 2002, when I served in that beautiful country ravaged by the greed bought about by the supply and demand of the 'blood diamond'. The illegal diamond trade in Africa is rife; diamond mines in the northern districts are guarded heavily by barbaric, ruthless employees of the West. For the locals forced to work the mines, life is cheap. I remember the dead bodies left lying in the gutter in the middle of Freetown – any claim on corpses meant that those picking them up must pay for their removal and burial. Families couldn't afford to claim their lost children, so they were left roadside until the smell became unbearable. My initial three months were relatively easy, but then I moved upcountry as part of a small military observation team. We travelled everywhere: Makeni, Kenema, and Bo were just a few of the many places we went. The eerie sound of the Mi-24 Russian Hind gunship above made for some interesting evenings. (The Hind is likened to, and sometimes preferred over, the AH-64 Apache.) The children of any war-torn country always affect me the most, and I dealt with a lot of child combatants in Sierra Leone – the youngest was just seven.

His story remains permanently fixed in my mind, and I often wonder what became of him. The rebels who kidnapped him forced him to kill his entire family; this was his initiation. How do you heal a youngster who has been through such physical and mental trauma? Young girls taken were used as sex slaves. We Brits engaged in very successful operations in Sierra Leone; however, we waited far too long before we intervened, just as we always do.

Hootie and the Blowfish saw me through the summer of 2003 in Iraq, and Snow Patrol kept me sane during my first tour of Helmand in 2006. Even now, the tracks ping so many memories, good and bad. Bob Dylan, the Rolling Stones, and Creedence Clearwater Revival are fundamental albums on tour.

Music is an important part of my life, and every experience, good or bad, has a soundtrack. It provides me with a way to come to understand things – at the very least, it gives me the means to try to put things into perspective. If I could have chosen a path for myself, it would have been that of a singer or songwriter, or perhaps both. I used to write lyrics and poetry as a child. The poetry grew darker through my teenage years, and I now put much of that down to the haze that engulfed me through my abuse of cannabis. The writing stopped when I was in my early twenties, as did the cannabis use. I've already shared how I forced myself out of 'shitsville' and on to the army careers office, but I didn't describe music's impact on the decision. The truth is, when I realised that I didn't sound much like Sheryl Crow, I opted to join the army instead, and then becoming a combat medic was just the best fit for me. Lying on my stretcher in the CAP, still clad in my blood-stained, filthy combats, I know that I made the right decision.

I let my thoughts go, turning my attention back to the ongoing banter. The Crows are the focus of much discussion, and it's not long before I am also pinged to marry the interpreter that I spooned with in order to keep warm during our first night in the PB.

Kev initiates this with, 'Puttin' oot on the first date, eh, mucker?'

Rolling over on my stretcher and turning my back on Monty is against all of my better judgement, leaving my precious speaker vulnerable, but I do it anyway. Letting my eyelids drift shut to rest my eyes for a second, I suddenly hear Michael Buble bellowing out of my speaker. 'What the fuck is this? Are we in a shopping centre? Is it Christmas?' I shout out.

Monty laughs before grabbing my speaker, guaranteeing that it's out of reach of me. He tries in vain to defend his own collection of Buble swing.

'Nice! Just the type of banging tunes we expect from a Scottish warrior, Monty.'

Within minutes, the Crows are back on. Already in hard cover, we continue to sprawl out on the stretchers and roll mats on the floor. Laughing, we make fun of the different events that have taken place over the past few months.

Then, without warning, our jovialities are interrupted. We all freeze for a second, as rounds start zipping through the blacked-out windows of the room we are in. A single round ricochets off the old blackboard and then bounces around on the floor in front of me. Monty starts laughing. It's more of a nervous 'what the fuck is that?' laugh. We all pause, as still as the 'dog statues' that we saw on the first night: where else can we take cover? The walls are hardened, and we are already on the ground.

I start laughing at Davey's quick reactions; he moves like a stunned gazelle. We roll about cackling like children, happy in the knowledge that the rounds didn't hit anyone. This began to get outrageous, and clearly we were getting a natural high from the adrenaline rush. It's strange, but you get so used to rounds bouncing around that it doesn't bother you the way it should.

The barrage peters out, and I start what eventually becomes a daily ritual: I roll and smoke a cigarette. It signifies the end of the day, and it gives me something to look forward to. Tobacco is far easier to pack than cigarettes; my emergency supply for moments like this has found itself a new home: the map pocket in the side of my combat trousers.

I wasn't a regular smoker prior to this 'atmospherics' check on Nad-e Ali, a social smoker if I smoked at all, and now here I am smoking roll-ups like a hippie. Everybody is busy establishing their own workable routine of eating, sleeping, fighting, or bleeding. The gaze of a rabbit in headlights has faded. All the guys know the importance of rest and routine, so we all look forward to the peace that the night-time brings.

Sgt Maj. Robertson and I make plans to start a daily walk round; we cover all the positions on the outer perimeter. It's to check on morale of the troops more than anything. Davey asks me to check in on young Freddie McCabe, one of the junior soldiers cut off earlier today.

Monty confirms that Freddie isn't acting himself. 'He's quiet, Channy. Not sure why.'

Young soldiers are never quiet; they have an energy that seems to go on and on. Freddie's commander, Tam, was shot while trying to help the two young Jocks who were cut off during a firefight. On paper, reaction to contact works perfectly; in reality, you'll find the nearest cover and drop into it. The last thing on your mind is keeping in a neat, regimental straight line. No one wants to be the guy suffering mentally, and no one wants to ask for help. At his age, Freddie is going through a lot more than many of his peer group at home. He, too, could have chosen a very different path. A fan of hardcore dance music and cans of Red Bull, he reminds me of Duffy.

I ask him for a quick chat. He is reluctant at first, but I force him into it. 'You can talk to me or one of the docs back in Camp Bastion,' I tell him.

These situations can be easier for a female medic to deal with because sometimes men worry that they will be judged if they show any weakness. When you are 18 and fighting this hard, your friends falling beside you, sometimes you need that cup of tea and a chat. I recognise that I may be morphing into my grandmother with the whole 'cup of tea' thing. 'Right, so you have had both your legs blown off and could potentially lose a ball sack, how about a nice cup of tea and a digestive biscuit?'

Straight-faced, I explain the scenario to Freddie.

Laughing, he replies, 'I wouldn't mind the conversation if the tea was replaced with a Red Bull.'

He gestures for us to sit down on a bench outside the aid post. Freddie doesn't need me to patronise him, so rather than beat around the bush, I just ask him straight up what happened, and then I let him do the talking.

'We got fuckin' hit, so me and Duffy hit the deck. I looked over and saw rounds comin' down the middle of the track between us and the rest of the multiple. They (the Taliban) musta had a fuckin' gun position on the fuckin' path.' He relays the details, describing the incident and the feeling of panic at being cut off from his platoon. 'Tam just came out of nowhere to our position, the mad cunt coulda been killed,' he adds.

Reminding him of the events when the WMIK got cut off, I explain that it's normal to be freaked out. Making light of the situation, we joke that he may have shit his pants just as Duffy had said he had done, not literally of course.

'I have no spare pants that I am willing to part with, Freddie.'

Smiling, he responds, 'Cheers for the offer, but I'll live, eh.'

I make a joke about the difficulties of doing our laundry, and he laughs. The small detail of washing the clothing that I am living in is something I always do under the radar, never wanting the entirety of the PB to see my underwear hanging on a washing line; black field undies are inappropriate visual aids. The three of us – Jen, Abbie, and I – are cut from the same cloth: we all place our underwear underneath the T-shirts that we wash. It's a strange ritual, I know, but, looking back, I am glad that we kept our dignity, if nothing else.

Freddie laughs again as I continue the conversation about my own struggles, a quick switch fire so that he will forget his own. It works. My shifting the focus to myself helps to make light of the situation. We talk for about ten minutes about my washing routine, including my yellow sharps container. I ask if he would like to borrow it, and he declines. I reassure him that all of us are in new territory, regardless of how many years we have served. Fear is healthy, and that's what probably kept him alive.

I add, 'All of my tours could be described as relatively tame compared to this one.'

He laughs when I remind him about Duffy. The thought of Duffy now back in Lashkar Gah, annoying people again with his hardcore dance music, makes me smile.

Ferris struts past as we are finishing up, shouting, 'Man the fuck up, Freddie!'

Freddie replies, 'Get te fuck, ya prick.'

This alone tells me that Freddie will be just fine; the best therapy comes from those who you share the experience with. 'Ferris therapy' wins again; not allowed to dwell too much, Freddie returns the favour by just cracking on.

I know that many of the soldiers here are nursing thoughts

of getting injured, and, worse still, of getting killed. We all think about the days and weeks ahead. With our friends evacuated daily back to Camp Bastion, our numbers are diminishing rapidly; we have lost at least a multiple worth of men, with a running score of about fifteen, including command elements. It's not a great feeling, but it is something we all share and try to ignore.

When we get back to the UK, we will talk to other soldiers about our experiences, if we talk about them at all. In the past, I tried to describe certain situations to friends at home, but they unintentionally look bored. Maybe it's my storytelling ability! In any case, I proceeded to talk to my drink of choice for that evening, enjoying its response far more than that of my friends. This is just the way it is.

I don't have the luxury of thinking about my own experiences for long – there's work to be done. Good news from Lash brightens the mood. We are getting a resupp tonight, along with the OMLT for the Afghans; they should have been here days ago, but like so many things in this part of the world, they have been delayed. Monty will also get a platoon commander.

The OMLT are drawn mainly from the Royal Irish Regiment (RI); when they arrive, they will work and live among the Afghans. We know from past experience that rogue Afghans have taken guns to British and American troops several times. It's a job that I would not relish, and I admire the troops that do it.

The day passes without incident, and everyone looks forward to the resupp. I do a little personal administration: clean my weapon, wash my smalls, carry out the underwear-under-the-T-shirt drill, and dust my feet with powder. I am looking forward to the introduction of some new rations; the same old choice is killing me. I am desperate to taste something other than mashed-up steak and vegetables. I am also conscious of the fact that my arse is in danger of being on display to the general populace of the base: the thin material is wearing away. My combats are covered in blood and grime and in desperate need of a wash; even the boss has commented on my state in general 'Sgt T, it looks like you've gone feral.' He's right.

Everyone's kit is in turmoil; hopefully, the medics back at Lash have packed up some stuff for the four of us medics out here, and this will be sent down on the helo as part of the resupp. I know that I can rely on the team at Lash, and for a moment, I miss the banter back in the medical section.

I briefly wonder if they know what is going on out here, and I am sure that they have had their own casualties to worry about. We had a fair few ourselves back early on this tour. The MOB was aptly named 'mass casualty central', as large numbers of locals pass through the aid station en route to the Bost Afghan hospital.

The atmosphere around the PB is buzzing now. The resupp is the first bit of good news that we have received in the last six days. The RI team from the OMLT will take some of the pressure off the boss, especially when it comes to the handling of the Afghans. They will now have a full team to mentor them out on the ground.

Looking after yourself and your team can be challenging, but directing a patrol of Afghans, many of whom seem to mince around with their safety catch off, is a major concern... at least for me, anyway.

I ask Abbie to calculate our casualty figures while we adjust some of the kit in the medical room.

She shouts out, 'Thirty! We have evacuated thirty casualties!' Her calculations have surprised her.

Even now, I struggle to remember them all. It's like the past six days have been a blur. I try to recap all of the injured, but I can't actually remember them. I look at the book... evacuated thirty casualties in six days? I am not bothered by that particular number. It's just that I realise that we are here for the next two months, so what on earth does the future hold?

I check the stock list that I have made and start to think about other items that may become useful. I write down anything that comes to mind; the majority of it involves bleed kits. Not a fan of medics playing God, I like to evacuate our seriously injured quickly. I have no replacement blood to give, and casualties are always going to be better off when they reach Camp Bastion. It's not a time for me or my medics to start experimenting with our skills. Identifying the need for early surgery is a skill that we as a brigade have mastered very well, and we use it to great effect.

Our drill is clear. Only make limb-saving or lifesaving interventions, and leave the rest to the surgeon's knife. B Company and the Afghans are being hit hard. I notice one thing in myself and the others on day six. We as soldiers are no longer bothered by the situation in which we now find ourselves. Even the last-light attacks have become a bit of a circus.

If it only took six days to become hardened to the ferocity of war. How long would it take for us soldiers to recover from the emotional scars that combat will inflict on us? British troops, along with the Americans, have sustained many casualties and endured heavy fighting in both Afghanistan and Iraq. Where do we go next? I believe that the psychological impact on our soldiers has yet to be measured.

I have read and learnt from older colleagues that combat stress was high in Northern Ireland during the troubles that spanned across decades from 1969 to the late 1990s. In Ulster at the height of the violence, the fear of being shot dead in a sniper attack created a huge psychological impact on young soldiers. The Iraq campaign delivered a new kind of fear of being captured and beheaded by insurgents.

These modern-day conflicts are not like the battles of the great wars; they, too, were mentally and physically draining of course, but the soldiers knew that in the main, if captured, they would be sent to a POW camp. Afghanistan and Iraq offer no such assurances; they are barbaric. The Taliban will hang a pregnant mother and cut her open in the street if they think she has spoken to coalition forces; troops on the ground will carry that visual forever.

Post-traumatic stress disorder (PTSD) has been prevalent for many years among those who have served. Military life has always encouraged a heavy drinking culture, and we, the British public, live in a society dominated by alcohol. This is fine in moderation. For many men and women coming home from conflict and having experienced hardship or situations which have affected them mentally, it can be a struggle to integrate back into normal life.

Mundane tasks without routine can be difficult, and problems often go unnoticed. The more time that you spend in a uniform, the more institutionalised you become. My family noticed changes in me when I came home from previous tours, and my lack of patience would sometimes cause me to act irrationally. I recall standing in line in a cobbler's shop when the man in front of me seemed to take an age over what he wanted. He kept repeating himself time and time again. I could feel myself getting angry, and before I could do anything to check myself, I found myself gripping him for taking too long. The way I spoke to him was unacceptable, but at the time I didn't comprehend what I was saying. He looked taken aback. As I stormed out of the shop, I felt embarrassed and wondered what had come over me. In hindsight, I try to pinpoint if my PTSD was from personal or professional trauma; I definitely suffered far more mentally from the death of my brother. PTSD is not just for those who have been to war; in some cases, the support network is non-existent in the civilian world because the signs are not recognised as quickly.

Striving to do well all of my life, I had become overefficient at everything, almost robotic. I was obsessed with getting tasks done at warp speed, ensuring that I was straight to the point about everything. My phone manner was boorish, rebuking sales advisors over my inefficient phone contract or berating the banking phone service about unknown transactions. I was wearing myself out, and, worse still, I was wearing my family out.

I recognised what I was doing; fortunately, I come from a household where there is no problem letting you know if you are acting like an arsehole. Words from my father etched into my brain: 'You ain't the sergeant major in this house.' *Roger that, Dad.* I toned down my enthusiasm to three-quarter warp speed. I had always been motivated, that was part of my charm, so it wasn't all down to PTSD.

I just had to consider my tone and stop publicly chastising people. The shoe guy was lucky that tar and feathering was no longer acceptable.

Relating very much to the film *Falling Down* with Michael Douglas, I identified the build-up and eventual breakdown of people in countries that are falling into a quagmire of hatred. When our fallen come home and are at risk from protest and disruption, or our soldiers are called murderers and child killers as they march through their home towns, it angers me.

I force myself back to the present, a bit jangled by mental digression. I know that we will all have to face PTSD and other waking nightmares once we return home; having gone through it all before, it is hard not to think about it. But focusing on the tasks at hand is necessary, for the guys I support as much as for me.

Time draws close to the eagerly awaited inbound flight. It's after midnight, and the HLZ is secured and ready to receive. The Chinook lands and begins to drop off its load.

'One, two, three, four, five, and six.' I count the crates for Davey as they come off.

The helicopter isn't down for long, and it quickly takes off under the cover of darkness. A gopping mouthful of dirt for me as a souvenir of the helo's departure. Great... my teeth are sticking to my lips, and unless I get to some water soon, that is the way that they will stay. This is as bad as having furry teeth, perhaps worse, but I will crack on in spite of it.

Davey calls for the all-terrain vehicle (ATV) and trailer to come. They arrive quickly, and everyone mucks in to help offload the pallets. We all notice the clean-looking soldiers helping; they must be the overdue OMLT.

Hearing the unmistakable tones of someone who can only be an officer, I get eyes on the back of a floppy blond mop of hair. He sounds like he must be a Guards officer, very well spoken and using an abundance of dialogue to relay information that could be understood better using sign language. The young Jocks look on, ignoring him in the hope that he is talking to someone else. The officers of 5 Scots are rough around the edges, and that is absolutely cool with me; they don't lack intelligence, they just know how to handle their men, no pomp and no ceremony. This is as it should be with grunts, and they like it that way.

Proper introductions with the new arrivals will wait until tomorrow; it's late, and my roll mat is calling my name loudly. The boss declares a no-patrol day tomorrow, so everyone can get some rest. I settle down to another restless night's sleep, and it is not long before the brightest of suns initiates another early start. My unkempt hair is slowly turning into dreadlocks, and I am aware that I smell funkier with each passing day. I note how clean the OMLT are, compared to the rest of us, but rest assured that it won't be long before they are just as dishevelled as we are.

These guys have already been involved in heavy fighting up north. I wonder how they will compare their past experience to life in Nad-e Ali. The arrival of the OMLT reminds me of the RI soldiers that served with the brigade in the summer of 2006. I think about Spence, a colour sergeant (CSgt) who taught me a hard lesson during a tactics cadre at the infantry training centre in Wales (ITC Brecon). He was injured in the Sangin Valley back in 2006, and he gave me an unexpected appreciation of the ferocious (or teeth-arm) soldiers that I would be supporting on future operations. In one particular training attack, I was appointed the number two on the GPMG, also called the 240.

I was part of a two-man gun team, and my role was to assist the gunner by carrying extra ammo. Initially, I thought that I had a much easier task than going forward as one of the assaulting section. I can still recall my own smugness as to the easy role I had been given. One effort up onto the high ground, and then all I had to do was place myself into a fire support position until the enemy had been cleared, feed my gunner rounds while lying on my belt buckle giving over watch to the assaulting section and looking for fall of shot for my gunner. *How hard could that be?* I thought at the time. How wrong I was.

It was only a matter of minutes before I found out all about my colossal misjudgement, and here started the lesson that I now reflect on. It's simply this: no one gets an easy job when it comes to fighting. Everyone in the platoon had already endured a long tactical advance to battle (TAB), and everyone was hanging out (that is, physically exhausted). When we came under effective enemy fire, the platoon advanced and began to close on the enemy. Gun teams began to move into positions on the high ground, including me and my gunner.

CSgt Spence decided to prematurely kill off my gunner, which left me carrying the heavy machine gun, my own weapon, and all the machine guns rounds (or 'link', as we call it) that we were carrying between us. 'Not so easy anymore, eh, Sgt Taylor?' he shouted.

My eyes said it all as I shuffled along before falling heavily into a fire support position; the DS (instructors) tried hard not to laugh as they watched me. Pretending that I was absolutely fine, I dug deep to try not to show any signs of pain as my body smashed against rocks that were almost too well placed.

Feeling like both of my lungs were collapsing, I continued to engage the enemy. Only when the reorg (or 'regroup', a term used to pause and replenish ammo and await the next order) was called at the end of the assault did I wish to be a part of the assaulting section – to be honest, I really wished that the exercise would come to an end. Any plausible excuse that did not involve my having to run from my location to the enemy position would have been welcome. It was one of the hardest things that I had ever done physically. The sheer weight of all of my kit made me vomit a little down the front of my smock. Why hadn't I tried harder to expend more ammunition? I searched for any reason that would make my kit lighter.

During the course run by the junior division, I had a little taste of what an infantry soldier does, and I am more than happy not to taste it again. Anyone who has spent any amount of time in the Brecon Beacons of Wales will appreciate how hard the infantry get it. That's why most of them have a bit of an attitude. I would too if I had to go through junior and senior command courses down there. I was one of three females who were the first to attempt the all-arms infantry tactics cadre. Coming from three very different backgrounds – combat medic, artillery sergeant, and a military police SNCO – all three of us made our mark. Passing with distinction before being awarded the honour of top student, I was glad to have the chance to learn more about low-level tactics. (I would be gladder still later on when those lessons saved my life.)

My days in the cadre were a lot like my current time with B Company in many ways. Over the last four months, I have gotten to know our company pretty well. I've chatted at length about my background and experience with Davey, who consistently sees humour in the strife and hardship that I've opted to undertake.

'Why do you do that shite to yourself, Channy?' he always says.

'Who knows, Davey? It's something that feels natural to me,' I always reply, reflecting the truth of my misspent adolescence.

As we sit talking, Davey is relieved to find that there's a warrant officer in the OMLT group. Tony Mason of the RI Regiment is quite a character. He certainly has the luck of the Irish, along with a contagious smile, both of which will see him and his crew through some rough times. When you see his smile, it makes you smile, and before long, everyone is smiling – about nothing.

Monty's new platoon commander arrives in the shape of 2Lt Du Boulay, straight out of Sandhurst and in-country for just a few weeks. I am unsure how a brand-new officer will survive out here; 2Lt Barclay, who had gathered some experience during the early months of the tour, shone brightly during his short stay here. Du Boulay will soon alleviate any doubts about his ability; in fact, he ultimately proves to be one of the finest officers that I have ever served with. (He, too, would be recognised for his bravery, receiving a mention in *Dispatches* for his courage and leadership under fire.)

Finally getting eyes on the voice from the night before, I am not surprised that he resembles Flashheart, the fictional World War I flying ace from *Blackadder*, the BBC comedy series. Just as I am thinking this, Ham McLaughlin comes into the ops room, asking straight away, 'Who the fuck is that, Flashheart from *Blackadder*?' We laugh because it's true: the officer is tall and a little awkward in his own skin, plus he has that mop of floppy blond hair that I've already described. Much like Flashheart, his attempts to make friends and influence people fail miserably. To put it bluntly, he is a snob, and I think some of the officers are slightly embarrassed by his behaviour. He's regularly reassured in no uncertain terms as to where he falls in the chain of command.

In a combat environment, it's important to have your share of every type of personality, just to keep things interesting. Flatliners make for boring battle buddies. Flashheart – I often thought of him as simply 'Flash' – did bring some morale in the shape of a red iPod. The blokes made great use of it, and not on account that his music taste was awesome. The red iPod is well stocked with a variety of 'alternative' entertainment. Suffice to say that with Flashheart leading the kandak into battle, it was all about to get a little more interesting.

The boss's plan for a no-patrol day is welcome and relaxing. We get stuck into the medical room and unload the new medical kit that has arrived. Weapons are cleaned, and the lads are taking full advantage of getting some extra sleep. Everyone struggles to sleep in the heat of the day, but sometimes just lying in some shade while swimming in your own sweat is better than nothing at all.

We are not let down when it comes to last light, as the

Taliban give their usual show of force. The only difference today is the introduction of the PKM, a Russian-designed 7.62 mm machine gun with an effective range of 1,000 metres. It's the Taliban equivalent of our own GPMG. I visualise the Taliban soldier eating his scoff before firing random bursts in our direction, just as a show of force and thankfully not accurate.

Orders are late today, and with everyone gathered in the ops room, it's time to discuss naming the PB. This is something that all units do; it easily identifies the PB when it comes to mapping and the like.

Forty minutes later, it's no surprise that the PB is named Argyll, on account of the soldiers defending it.

The base will soon be enjoying the peace that darkness brings. The place is always in complete blackout during night hours, reminding me of my own stupidity of smoking during our early evacuation.

Plans are already on the table in the ops room for operations tomorrow. Monty and I discuss what he needs medically. He takes Abbie with him, and the OMLT have Sean until their patrol medic turns up. Jen and I cover the medical post here, realising in the early days that you can't just put everyone out on the ground all of the time. The base has the safest area for helicopters to land, and my medics need someone with skills in advanced treatment to send their wounded back to. Maj. Clark needs sound advice and quick answers about casualties.

Our system makes certain that no casualty is ever left waiting. The base only has a basic set-up, but it affords our guys a safe haven. They know that we will be waiting for them, and it reassures them that we will deploy to them without question if they can't make it back.

Making my way to my bed space, I look forward to a sound night's sleep. The removal of my boots reveals the state of my socks, reminding me that our resupp of personal kit still hasn't arrived. I am surviving on two pairs each of pants and socks. I've always kept a backup pair of each in the bottom of my grab bag, and I am very thankful for that now. Little things like this make life more tolerable; another day done and dusted. Placing my earphones in, I fall asleep to the sounds of my top-rated tunes, thinking about home and getting there in one piece.

All too soon there's movement outside; it's not even first light as the blokes start to prepare to roll out. We all share some idle chat before they set off. I give Abbie and Sean the normal 'stay safe' routine. One thing that I always do is leave nothing left unsaid. Life changes very quickly out here, and you can easily find yourself wishing that you might have said more. A 'stay safe' is better than nothing.

I feel responsible for Abbie, Sean, and Jen – not just because I am the lead medic, but also because all three of them are younger than I am. If anything were ever to happen, I would have to explain myself when I faced their loved ones. It would be naive to think that they could never be one of the ones to get hurt. That is something I don't even like to think about, so I push it to the back of my mind, trusting my 'stay safe' to do its job. Watching as Sean and Abbie patrol off into the distance, I soak up the quiet they have left behind.

Soon it's *too* quiet. I decide to take a walk around the gun positions to check in with the blokes, knowing it's a welcome break for the Jocks on the wall to have someone else to talk to. First, though, I must put in my 'breakfast order'. We have taken to collecting breakfast rations in the ops room and cooking them in one of the many used ammunition tins. It's Kev's turn, so I hand him my boil-in-the-bag breakfast of sausage and beans before heading off on my checks. I put on my body armour and helmet and then make my way to the outer wall. This is the safest way to walk round, as it offers limited cover from any stray rounds flying around the base.

I chat to the Jocks who are awake and those preparing to change over their guard shift. They ask all the usual questions: How long are we here for? When is the next resupp? Who's the new bouffant-haired officer with the OMLT? This last refers to Flashheart of course. Ham has already given the blokes the low-down. The young Jocks don't hold back about anything or anyone. Their humour is the one thing that never leaves them, even at their lowest point. I am positive that the end of the world could be inbound, and these Jocks would still be taking the piss out of someone.

I finally get to the last position, and it's bathed in bright sunshine. The radio net is peaceful for a change. I notice that something isn't right: the soldier guarding it is asleep.

'What the fuck?' I say, putting my thoughts into words. As I shake him violently, he shunts forward. I recognise him as the armourer. He comes to quickly as I wade into him with some verbal encouragement in the form of, 'What are you on, you fucking prick? Wankers like you are why grunts trust no one but their own!'

He replies with, 'Uh, uh, uh, uh.' I can see that he is in a confused state, which further confirms the fact that he was asleep.

Davey, who is in charge of the security of the base, wastes no time involving himself heavily in the situation. We are in Taliban-held Nad-e Ali, and the thought of the base getting breached didn't even bear thinking about. It would be carnage. Short of shooting one of your own, this is as bad as it gets on operations. Davey goes ballistic! His boys have been getting thrashed, and this clown has only been on stag (or 'watch', as the

Americans call it) for half an hour. Dragging the soldier from his post, he says, 'You, son, come with me.'

The armourer climbs down. 'Sorry, sir,' he says as they move around the corner.

Discipline has to be Davey's business: there are no training instructors out here to put right mistakes, just enemy soldiers waiting to take advantage of them. Returning from their 'chat', the armourer appears stone-faced; his duty has been extended from two hours to six, so he picks up extra duties. Whatever Davey said or did must have done the trick, because from that day on, the armourer was never found asleep again while on stag. His punishment brings joy to the Jocks in his corner as they snigger out of sight of Davey. After all, Jocks will be Jocks, and laughing at someone else getting thrashed is a feeling I recall myself when I was a junior soldier. In fact, I remember doing it not so long ago in the sergeants' mess, so some things never change.

Jen and I now turn our attention to washing ourselves as best we can. I go through the normal daily rigour of thigh burn in the back of one of the wagons. My teeth are clean, and I am good to go. Scoff is cooking away, and I look forward to my sausage and beans. We look about for any menial tasks that need doing.

The morning goes by without incident. The men in Monty's platoon have been clearing compounds, and there are two other call signs in our area. The OMLT are conducting low-level ops with the kandak, and there's a police mentor unit en route from Lash. They are heading to the other compound, 'Sterling Lines', nearby with the police.

Unexpectedly, there are three loud explosions, followed by the sound of heavy machine gun bursts; it's all close by. The radio net goes crazy, and the base is silenced. Capt. Wood checks in with Monty, and he reports no activity from the enemy. He then checks in with Flashheart, again reporting no enemy activity.

We soon learn that the Throatcutters' call sign has been ambushed on their way into our area. One of their vehicles has taken a direct hit from an RPG. They are under heavy fire and have taken multiple casualties. It's just me and Jen in the medical room, so we know that we are going to be up against it. We prepare ourselves and then initiate the nine-liner early in order to warn Camp Bastion that we have several casualties inbound.

It takes at least fifteen minutes for the wounded to appear at our gate. There are four guys badly injured, one of them more severely than the others. An Afghan special ops soldier is KIA (killed in action). We cross-deck the injured and then get to work.

The Afghans bring the dead soldier in, placing him in the middle of the room. I realise that they think he is still alive; this does not seem likely to me, and even if he is still alive, he is not likely to last long. He has been shot through the head, so there's blood everywhere. (The head and face are typically vascular areas, which means they result in profuse bleeding. A nosebleed, for instance, creates far more blood than you would imagine. All of this accounts for why people freak out with head wounds.) It's sometimes better if the blood comes out, as opposed to pooling inside, but this is clearly not the case with this poor soldier.

The Afghans gather around their dead soldier and start fussing about him. They check his airway and try to move him. It's hard to watch them desperately trying to wake him. During the final stages of death, the body can produce spontaneous movement, which they take to be signs of life. Having already seen that half of his head is missing, I know that nothing can be done. I have the unfortunate task of pronouncing the soldier dead. It's not the norm, but we have no doctor to do it. I quickly make interventions on my own casualty and then move to the Afghan soldier. I check for signs of life: there's no output whatsoever, and his pupils are fixed.

I feel for the other Afghans who surround his body. It's their comrade and friend lying there, and they don't want to believe that he can't be helped. The Afghans deal with their dead in their own way, so I suggest that they take his body to prepare him for the MERT flight. I try to be as gentle as possible with them, as I know they feel the loss the same as we would.

I spot a familiar face from the police mentoring team in Lash; it's a relief to see that he is okay. He helps us tend to the wounded as we prepare our own for evacuation. These guys already received basic first aid on the ground. We recheck the tourniquets and make sure that fractured limbs are splinted. The skin is partially peeled back on one. I look at the injury with interest, noting, *Ah, that's what the radius and ulna look like, still intact and surrounded by blood vessels.*

The boss peers around the corner of the doorway. He looks at the carnage before him, and I can see he is taken aback. He gives me a sort of nod of appreciation. I understand that he needs information fast to relay over the net back to brigade HQ. He is being as diplomatic as the situation will allow. Maj. Clark is under pressure from brigade HQ and Camp Bastion, as they want information. This in turn will allow them to make their decisions and warn relevant surgeons to prepare for the wounded.

I have no plans to keep these boys for long. An orthopaedic surgeon will be far more useful than Jen or I. I make the call that they are stable enough to fly. Giving me the nod, the boss disappears into the ops room next door.

We have four casualties, plus another three with less-obvious wounds. Blasts often cause tertiary injuries in people close to the explosion, so these guys need to be evacuated as well. I can't risk recalling the MERT for slow-developing chest injuries, as intelligence, along with very recent ICOM chatter that has been intercepted, is giving some worrying information about the Taliban's future intentions and targets. So the number of casualties goes up from four to seven, plus one KIA.

The MERT are en route, so we finish up and prepare to move them to the HLZ. It takes a lot of us to carry all the stretchers. Bearing in mind that numbers in the base are declining, blokes are woken from their rest periods to help. They get up without question, knowing that if they were the ones lying on the stretchers, every man here would get up to carry them to the helo. Soldiers will moan with the best of them until someone gets injured.

Given the unexpected bloody start to the day, I start wondering if that's our lot for today as we make it across to the HLZ, where we wait patiently for wheels down. I start thinking about stretchers and the fact that we are running short of them. I ask Davey to grab a stretcher off the Chinook, telling him I will do the same.

Wheels are down, and we start hauling the casualties on, including our dead. The handover is done, and I reach out to grab a stretcher. A member of the MERT gestures for me not to take it, catching me unawares. I mouth, 'Did that just happen?' I'm in no mood to be told by some RAF nurse that I am only allowed to take one stretcher, especially when she can replenish her stock upon her return to Camp Bastion. I wonder if maybe they have somewhere else to go first. We've got men on the ground, and I am running dangerously low; they won't be diverting this flight, as the lads are seriously wounded. I conclude she's being a jobsworth. If ever there was a time that I wanted to inflict violence on a complete stranger, this was it! *What the fuck?* I raged inwardly, snatching the stretcher out of her hand and aggressively pointing to the stretchers that we have just loaded on, including our dead.

The noise on a Chinook is loud, drowning out any words spoken. Emotions are running high, and in the desperate state we are in, I am angry that she thought her behaviour was appropriate.

Sprinting down off the ramp I take cover while the helo lifts off. *Aren't we supposed to be on the same side?* I think to myself, still very angry.

This is turning into a shit day. First the armourer asleep on stag, and now the stretcher police. Heading back to the base, I mutter a host of profanities.

One of the Brit mentoring team starts to tell me how he was on top cover just seconds before the Afghan soldier was shot in the head. They had just changed over! The guys are cleaning out the wagon which was covered in blood. The dead soldier's helmet was retrieved; unfortunately, part of his head was still in it. Davey decides to bury it as a mark of respect. All British soldiers are made aware of local Afghan customs prior to arriving in Helmand, so they know that if bodies or body parts are found, they should be buried in a respectful manner (as long as time and safety allow it).

I think that regardless of how mentally tough you think you are, when it's your guys who are bleeding, you feel pretty vulnerable. That's just how I feel today. My desire to not hear someone else's war stories has gone. I want to hear anyone else's story but my own. I am not interested in B Company's holding Nad-e Ali. The mission to get the turbine to Kajaki Dam couldn't be further from my thoughts. I feel dejected and uncharacteristically negative. I am angry that we are always on the receiving end. Every day, we keep getting hit; every other day, we keep taking casualties. We don't have the kit or capabilities to sustain any of it. Our Osprey body armour is not holding up to the job at hand. I invested in BlackHawk pouches that fitted the armour much better, and I am now thankful to have done so.

It suddenly dawns on me that all this agitation is covering up my concern about losing one of our own. Today's KIA was Afghan, but it could just as easily have been one of ours. I don't want to acknowledge the black body bags underneath the old desk in the corner of the aid post. B Company has grown close, and I have started to look at a lot of the guys as family.

I go back to the medical room: it's like a scene from a horror film, with blood everywhere after the treatment of the injured. Jen and I scrub it with what we have. We do this in silence of course, all very British and stiff upper lip. Sometimes saying nothing is better; a big fat discussion is the last thing we need.

There was more to come for the PMT, who had to make their way back to Lash after being smashed on the way in. Strangely enough, they were smashed on the way back out as well. They report back with casualties, but none are serious. When you think about them making the journey back, knowing they were probably going to get hit, it shows the kind of blokes they are. But that's what's expected, and all the guys do it without question.

We soon realise that the Taliban are cutting off our supply line, which is bad news. They litter most of our routes with IEDs, so road moves become impossible. Disruption can sometimes be a far more effective weapon than rockets. All of the wars in history tell you that.

Surprisingly, Monty's crew has been left alone, as has Flashheart's kandak. The Taliban have already had their success today. Later in the evening, we endure a small-arms attack, but compared to earlier events, it's pretty tame. The Taliban body count is already at thirty; somehow, though, their fighters still come.

Earlier in the tour the Americans flooded Garmsir, a town which lies on the southern tip of Helmand Province. They deployed more than two thousand US Marines in the form of 24 Marine Expeditionary Unit; together with A Company of 5 Scots, they drove the Taliban out of Garmsir. This forced the insurgents to find another route up to the Sangin Valley. Marjah and Nad-e Ali have thus become the Taliban's new 'highway to hell'. A moment no doubt played out to AC/DC, in my head anyway.

We welcome Monty's platoon back in to the base. They can't believe that they missed all the drama. There is a lot to talk about, and our room stays lively until around 2000 hours. Every roll mat in the base is full apart from the radio stag and the young Jocks manning the wall. We work a rotation to cover the radio net, doing two hours at night and two hours in the day. I am on death stag tonight, and it's hard to stay focused. Radio checks take place every fifteen minutes. I wonder if anyone in brigade HQ has actually woken up to the fact that we are in a world of shit down here. It seems that the turbine move up north is taking all of the news. The latest rumour is that 3 PARA will be sent down here to boost numbers and conduct offensive operations.

The Pathfinder (PF) Platoon are also rumoured to be conducting offensive ops in Marjah; this will hopefully smash the Taliban before they get to Nad-e Ali. I start to run through some ridiculous trains of thought whilst listening to the white noise of the radio. What if we get stuck out here or the marines somehow can't get in? What if the base gets overrun or one of our helicopters gets shot down? This is what happens when you get the radio watch in the early hours, the 'death stag'. I am pickling my own brain with this nonsense.

It's dark and quiet, so I keep a constant paranoid watch on the entrance to the makeshift ops room. Any shadows are starting to look like potential threats. My rifle is in my lap, barrel pointing towards the door. The longer I sit here, the worse it gets. An incident that took place up north in one of the FOBs suddenly hits my now-twisted psyche. One of the Afghan soldiers decided to fire a burst into a room where some of 2nd Battalion, Parachute Regiment (2 PARA) lay sleeping. He shot three of them; thankfully, none of them were killed – good time to think about it, though.

My stag is coming to an end, and it's definitely time for some bivvy bag action to clear the fuzziness out of my pan-fried head. Jen's on stag next, so it's time to wake her. Probably the worst sound that any soldier will ever hear is someone whispering, 'your stag!' I hated it when I joined up, and I still hate it now.

The white noise from the radio continues as I lay down my head, and it takes at least another hour before I doze off.

Me, Sgt Chantelle Taylor, Helmand Province, Afghanistan, 2008; my final tour

The Argyle and Sutherland Highlanders (5 Scots) a 'multiple' of fighting men also known as a platoon minus.

*The beloved Snatch Land Rover sitting behind
the preferred open-top WMIK.*

*My medical team, LCpl Sean Maloney, Pte
Abbie Cottle, me, and LCpl Jenny Young.*

Sgt Richard 'Monty' Monteith, B Company (5 Scots).

Lcpl Kev Coyle and me; 'battleshock' after our
first night on 'that roof' in Nade-Ali.

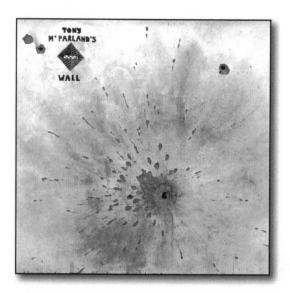

Afghan soldier 'Medi's' direct hit with an RPG;
unfortunately, Cpl Tony McParland got in the way.

My brother David and the lucky rosary beads,
kept in the inner sleeve of my body armour.

Casualty List (from 23 Aug 08)

23rd Aug 08 → x4 ANA — 1x GSW CHEST
                        1x MULTIPLE GSW
                        1x GSW ® ARM
                        1x GSW Ⓛ HAND

24 Aug 08 → x3 ANA 1xGSW BOTH LEGS
                        2x GSW ® ARM
         x 1 ISAF   RPG Ⓛ ARM Ⓡ HAND
         x 1 ANA   RPG SHRAPNEL TO
                        Ⓛ ARM

26 Aug 08 → ① x4 ISAF x4 RTA INJURIES
         x 1 ANA   x 1 KIA
         x 1 INT   RTA INJURIES
         x 2 INT   x 1 H/ATTACK
                        x 1 RTA INJ
         ① x 3 ISAF   x 1 GSW
                        x 1 EAR PERFORATION
                        x 1 BROKEN HAND

29 Aug 08 → x2 ISAF x 1 GSW
                        x 1 LIGAMENT
                        DAMAGE ANKLE

Original casualty list 1

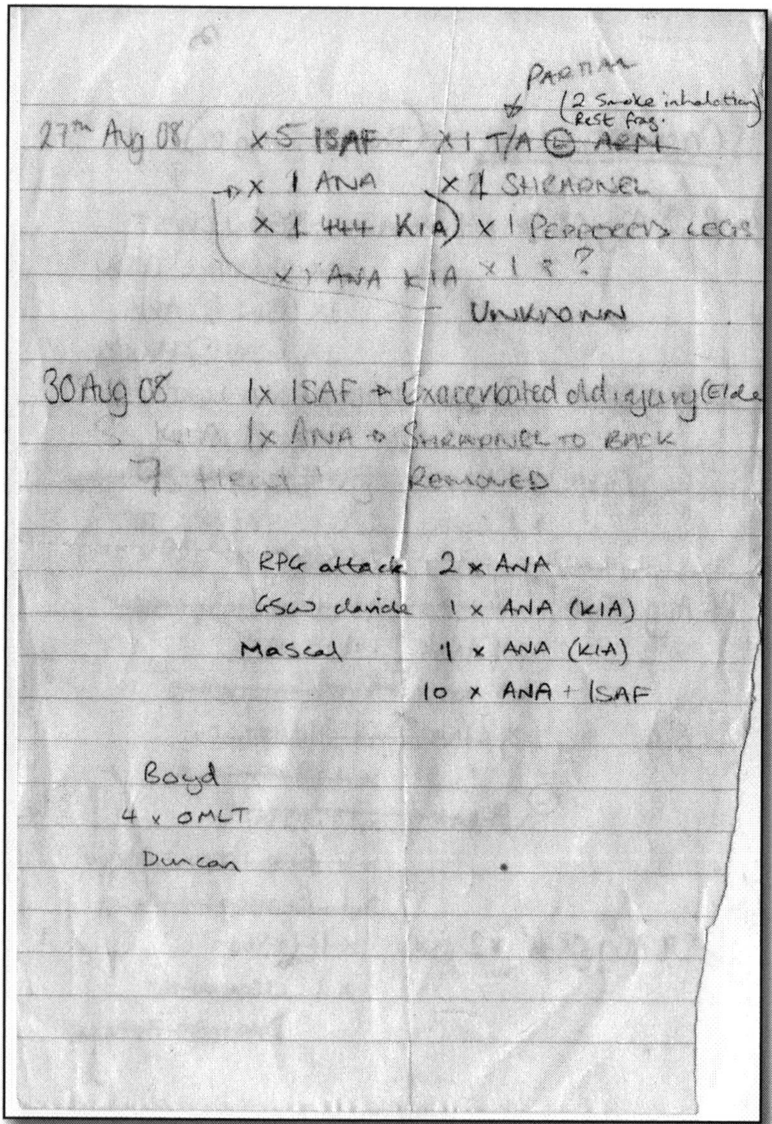

Original casualty list 2; paper was at a premium.

Sgt Scotty Mcfadden, B Company (5 Scots).

A grab bag of ammunition lies in front of my medical bag – we are soldiers who carry medical packs, not medics who carry weapons

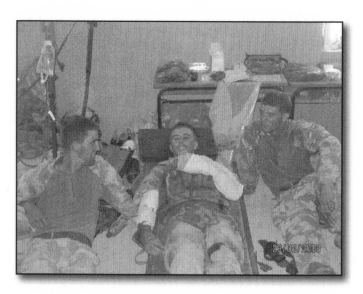

Cpl Tam Rankine flanked by his muckers before he is lifted – we made the four-hour deadline.

Cpl Scotty Pew's .50 gun position on the roof, under constant attack, giving every patrol eyes on potential threats, engaging with accuracy and speed.

Boydy, pre-gunshot wound.

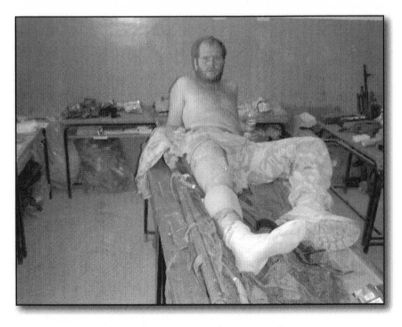

Boydy, post-gunshot wound.

The men of B Company, 'Holding Nade-Ali'.

The Helmand Diet' – best-kept secret in the world.

My telephone hub, below the .50 cal.

*Sgt Major Davey and I manning the
51 mm like a well-oiled machine.*

Cpl Stu Pearson receiving the QGM from our queen.
Stu suffered more than ten separate injuries from
the infamous mine strikes near the Kajaki Dam.

Cpl Mark Wright lost his life in the minefield
at Kajaki; he was awarded the George Cross
for his outstanding courage and bravery.

On the IED-littered canal road to Nawa district.

My good friend Sgt Phil Train (2 PARA).

My grandfather Buck Taylor of 'Baker Troop' 41 Independent Commando RM, leaving for a daylight combined RM/ US raid on the north-east coast of North Korea.

Life in the private sector has helped me understand the once-hated 'bigger picture'.

CHAPTER 5

FACE-TO-FACE WITH THE TALIBAN

OVERNIGHT, AS IF BY MAGIC, A SHOWER UNIT HAS APPEARED in the middle of the base. It looks like a tepee, the type of shelter you find at the Glastonbury music festival. Since our arrival, no one has been able to have a proper wash; most of us have taken to using my multipurpose yellow sharps container and a flannel or small cloth. I have gotten used to being grubby, and it no longer bothers me. Still, the shower is a welcome sight for all of us.

Kev and I sit quietly, relaxing in the ops room. Maj. Clark is enjoying his first shower, and Capt. Wood is reading outside. Daydreaming on my roll mat, I think about what may become of us down here. My moment of peace is interrupted by a conversation developing outside. Flashheart is discussing how the lack of amenities must be taking its toll on the men of B Company, worse still for the female soldiers who are attached. Kev looks at me with a smirk, already knowing that I will have something to say about it.

I ignore the conversation until the role of women on the front line is raised. Kev's smirk is now a full-on Cheshire cat grin. Smiling back, I acknowledge that I have heard Flashheart's comments but am far too relaxed to engage in shit chat with the man so early in the morning. I hold out for a whole two minutes, and then Flashheart appears in my peripheral vision. From the moment he arrived, I knew it was only a matter of time before he would start to annoy me.

'So, Sgt Taylor, what do you think?' he asks.

'About what, sir?' I reply.

'Females,' he says. 'Females serving in the infantry.'

I pause for a second, looking at the floppy-haired officer before me. I scan his kit and scrutinise the way he is dressed. I get eyes on two knee pads, one on each knee. No one ever wears two knee pads; you only need two if you are busy doing stuff you shouldn't be. I only packed one knee pad, and the rest of B Company has done the same. If he was defusing a bomb, maybe he would be forgiven, just like the dude in *The Hurt Locker* pulling up a daisy chain with his bare hands. (A daisy chain is a long line of any number of IEDs, usually initiated by one device or trigger, tactics used with devastating effect during the uprising in Iraq in 2004.) Flash reminds me of one of 'those soldiers', the type who will wear a full set of waterproofs just in case it rains – very much a precautionary operator, as opposed to a remedial one.

This told me all that I needed to know about Flashheart. Happy to engage in his shit chat, and without too much thought, I reply swiftly, my tone unwavering and with just a hint of sarcasm. 'From my own experiences, I am personally not keen on it; however, if it is about choice, roles should open up. There are plenty of weak individuals being carried already, though, aren't there, sir?'

Blushing slightly, he offers no comeback to my response. The only sound is laughter coming from our 2IC outside. Capt. Wood and I have forged a solid working relationship, and we've already had this conversation. He knows me and my team well and has come to rely on us, as we have him. We spent much time together in Nawa, a district to the north of Garmsir. He's a witty young officer undoubtedly destined for great things.

When I hear liberals having their often-heavy debates about equality in the armed forces, I think, *Send your daughter or sister to the front line; better still, send yourself, and soak up a bit of atmospherics in Nad-e Ali, Sangin, or Marjah; then you can make an informed decision.* There are women who have the stomach to push a bayonet into another person, twist it, take it out, and do it again and again, in order to be sure that the enemy is dead. Those types are a rarity; female soldiers already play a key role in many areas of the military: intelligence, technical areas, dog handling, command positions, fighter pilots, Apache gunship pilots, and, of course, combat medics. In Helmand, some of the bravest young soldiers are the females driving the unit supply trucks across the open desert. These convoys constantly face Taliban attacks. Of course there are also the women who serve with MERT.

In Afghanistan, women have been forced to squeeze into the front line because we have so few troops trying to stabilise the area. For many years, there were more than 20,000 British troops in Northern Ireland; yet, when we first deployed to southern Afghanistan, we sent just 4,500 troops, and it took several years before that was increased to 10,000.

As a military force, we simply cannot provide the safe and secure environment to allow reconstruction to take place. All the humanitarian efforts will be futile if the insurgency is allowed to continue and, in some cases, expand. The only way that the UK could have ever realistically delivered success in southern Afghanistan would have been to surge troops to at least 30,000. Then, in the early years, we might have been able to hold on to the ground that we fought so hard for. We name FOBs and PBs in memory of our fallen, yet do not have the good grace to keep hold of them. Our soldiers should never have been exposed to situations where they are so obviously outnumbered by the enemy.

I recall an incident back in 2006, when a small number of paratroopers remained isolated for more than a month in the district centre of Musa Qaleh. Against all odds, the men held the base, only to see it handed back to Taliban control six months later. How is that justified, and who makes the decision? With no strategic gain in handing it back, we as soldiers on the ground are left a little dispirited knowing that even the ever-so-important 'big picture' isn't gaining, either. We the Brits are trying to secure a country twice the size of Wales; never indifferent to the cause, we remain steadfast when the decision makers get it wrong. The UK government did not increase troop numbers to any significant level until 2008, perhaps through fear of losing public support. This may have been generated by concern that Britain would see more soldiers killed; in the end, the Americans came to our rescue. The lefties in Parliament are all but destroying the fabric of our society. We need a Churchill or Thatcher back in the top spot, the kind of Brit who knows how to take care of business overseas.

These are my views, and I'm not shy about sharing them. It's life or death for us here; there's no time for nonsense, and I have no patience for it, even when it's just shit chat. I'll give it right back to Flashheart again if the opportunity presents itself.

Relaxing again, I make a cup of tea. Abbie and Jen soon join me, and the three of us discuss the wish list of kit that should be arriving in the resupp. Just when I start thinking it's safe to chill out, Flashheart saunters into the ops room, holding what looks like a small French coffee press. 'Anyone for coffee?'

I look at Abbie, who in turn looks at Jen, and then all three of us look at Kev. A second later, the giggling starts. Shaking my head, I politely decline his offer, burying my head in my bivvy bag.

Flashheart makes his coffee, which he takes outside. He sits on the bench, sipping his coffee and smoking a Marlboro Lights cigarette. He looks just as comfortable here in Nad-e Ali as I'm sure he would sitting outside a pub in the West End of London. His annoying aura makes him quite interesting; I find myself watching him as he cuts about the place. This helps me pass the time and gives me something amusing to think about, a welcome respite from recent more-depressing thoughts.

The entertaining moment is interrupted as the radio net gets loud and busy. We hear a contact report from the Pathfinder call sign, which involves heavy fighting in Marjah, to our south. Quiet time is on hold as we listen to the drama unfold.

'We were lucky down there, mucker,' Kev says.

'I know, mate. Let's hope they are too,' I reply.

Neither of us says anything else, but I start thinking about our time in Marjah, part of which is described in the prologue. B Company had not long returned from the Nawa district, south of Lashkar Gah, when we were sent down to an unknown AO in Marjah. As the lead medic of B Company, I had deployed along with the command group. On top cover with Kev, we covered arcs like everyone else on our patrol. As a non-combatant, my role allowed me to protect myself and my patients. But modern warfare didn't see the Red Cross or Crescent as a sign of peace: we were targeted just like everyone else; if anything, we were seen as a weaker and easier objective for enemy fighters. My role on top cover was more about prevention than cure, as sitting in the back with no visual on the ground would have made me a very easy target. The road move to Marjah was a long and slow process. Every few hundred yards, we had to stop at what were considered to be vulnerable points (VPs) – that is, places the Taliban might attack from, or where they might plant IEDs. We had to get out and search the ground with mine detectors, checking for booby traps; this is a lifesaving process called 'Op Barma'. The drill was enforced at almost every VP. Nobody enjoyed the time-consuming task, but everyone understood the importance of it.

The week before our trip, we had lost three lads, along with a female soldier, so no one complained that we were being cautious. It was because members of our own company had been hit prior to our trip to Marjah that I came to be on these patrols in the first place: the company needed medical cover. Cpl Neil McKenzie, who was then B Company's lead medic, had been injured when he was thrown out of the WMIK that initiated a sizeable IED. He and a couple of others were extremely lucky to survive. That day, their open-top Land Rover earned its reputation as a better choice than the heavier armoured vehicles.

The heat from the sun made the journey unbearable at times. With nowhere to shelter, we were at the mercy of Afghanistan's cloudless blue skies. A trick I had learnt in the jungle of Sierra Leone helped to keep our water supply at a decent temperature. The key was to drench an old sock in water and then place the warm bottle inside of it. The warmth in the water evaporates into the sock, leaving the water relatively cool. It was a small luxury that made life in the desert bearable.

Initially, we stayed in the open desert outside of Marjah. Our mission was to probe and report on atmospherics and any unusual activity in the area. During intelligence briefs, Marjah had been identified as a haven for insurgents intent on the cultivation of poppies.

Our operation was set over several days. At night, we would use the desert as a makeshift base. It provided clear 360-degree arcs, so an all-round defence stance was adopted. On the first day of the patrol, I saw a suspect vehicle, full of what we considered fighting-age males. It went tearing past our convoy, between five hundred and six hundred metres away. It got everyone's attention and was a small combat indicator of what was yet to come. During dark hours, the general routine would normally be to rest around our vehicles, eating our scoff, covering radio stag after last light, and waiting for sunrise.

During the hottest part of the day, we would try to find shade, and in the middle of the desert that task can be interesting. I remember finding that the coolest place was down beside one of the Land Rover wheels; I somehow managed to squeeze my five-foot-eight-inch frame into that tiny shadow.

After several days, half the company was given orders to return to Lash; the rest of us would continue to probe in and around the outskirts of Marjah. That night, we took some IDF on our desert leger; it wasn't particularly close, but it felt like a warning to me. Besides, it was close enough to force us to move two kilometres (or clicks) away. We continued to probe, focusing our attention closer now in search of any signs of obvious enemy activity.

The heat was crippling at times, and my Sierra Leone trick had to stop: I couldn't justify the use of water to dampen the sock, so drinking hot water in extreme heat was a given – it was enough to make you vomit. It's hard to explain how or why exactly, but the heat, more than anything else, made patrols tough. When not on foot, we were in the vehicles, which were like ovens; it was soul destroying, and that was before anything kinetic even occurred.

Throughout our time in Marjah, I always felt that something

was going to happen; the longer we stayed, the stronger that feeling became. Orders came from higher command that we were to probe into the centre of Marjah.

The situation was not positive, and the mixture of excitement and fear was something that I was eager to release. My palms were sweaty, I was thirsty, and yet for some reason, I couldn't wait to get into Marjah.

We moved off slowly and purposefully, and it wasn't long before the first IED was discovered. The mine clearing equipment we use was based on the same principals as the machines used by enthusiasts that search for old coins and metals.

During our routine Op Barma drill, I recall saying to Kev, 'This isn't right.' Locals were in short supply, and the place was deserted. The smell of cooking reminded me of the time of day: it was getting close to lunch, and that meant the heat would keep increasing.

As we turned on to one of the tracks which led to the canal, I saw local villagers running – and they weren't running towards us, they were running away. I looked at Kev, saying, 'We are gonna get fuckin' smashed here.' Kev just laughed nervously. He knew I was right, and we both were just wondering where it would come from. Constantly scanning all around, all we could do was keep wondering what was going to happen.

My excitement had very positively disappeared, and the fear kicked right in. My legs felt like jelly. I now wanted something to happen just so I could feel or think about something else. The adrenaline shift had happened: I was again at that point where the anticipation was worse than the actual event.

Kev was my battle buddy on this mission. I trusted him implicitly and hoped that it wasn't us getting hit first. 'IED or small arms?' I whispered to Kev. I didn't have to wait long for my answer.

Our patrol crawled onto the canal track and started to push slowly down the side of it. We had no choice; we were committed. Kev and I were in the second vehicle. The local villagers continued to run, and then the place erupted. *Boom! Boom!* Two deafening explosions were followed rapidly by small-arms fire and heavy machine guns. The familiar airburst of incoming RPGs rained debris and shrapnel all around us.

Our patrol came to a grinding halt. Kev and I were shunted forward into the metal ledge in front of us, taking sustained and heavy fire from every direction. Smoke began to fill the air, making it hotter than before, if that were possible. Rounds started pinging off the top of our vehicle, and I remember seeing them zip through the antenna above me. Within seconds, the mounted guns on our WMIKs roared into action; the sound was unbelievable.

Kev and I had immediately taken cover, ducking down inside the hatch. Looking up, I could see that the rounds were coming in from left to right, from my side of the wagon. They zipped past so quickly that it made all of my own movements feel like I was in slow motion. I couldn't move fast enough.

Our vehicles could not withstand gunfire for long, so we had to react. I popped back up and immediately got eyes on a Taliban fighter: he was just over thirty metres away, half right of me in a field to our left. It happened very quickly. I engaged him, firing seven shots – good banter material for later: why was I wasting ammo? The first two were hazy. I just fired in his general direction, but then I could see him clearly, and I fired until he dropped. I could see his baggy clothing, which was darker than the colour of the field that he was standing in. His face was long, exaggerated by a straggly black beard. The one thing that struck me was the fearlessness in him: he wasn't looking directly at me, but he had to know the odds were he was about to die. He continued to fire elaborate bursts from his AK-47.

I shouted half a fire control order, but it wasn't anything like the ones that I had taught recruits to use. 'Half right, field,' was all that would come out. It was desperate, almost pathetic; I had the urge to point at the field. The noise was deafening, so words could not be heard. A hand signal seemed appropriate, and it got Kev's attention. The Minimi gunner in the vehicle behind us started engaging more fighters in the same field.

The fighter that I had engaged had already dropped, which meant that I could look to engage others. It would never be right to claim a kill as a medic; my job is to save lives. The fighter no longer had the ability to engage us, and that's all that concerned me. Faced with the choice of him or me, I chose me. I would still do the same.

The Taliban had timed their attack on us perfectly. They chose the hottest part of the day, which was just another tactic to slow us 'infidels' down; it would give them time to at least maim or kill a few of us.

'Man down! Man down!' I could hear the radio traffic through the back of the vehicle. The boss and driver were still in the front. 'One casualty in the rear vehicle, Sgt T,' Maj. Clark shouted through to the back, jumping out as I climbed through the back door of the vehicle to meet him.

From there, we started moving from cover to cover, making our way towards the rear of the patrol. We were vulnerable to enemy fire. I struggled beneath the burden of my heavy medical pack, the straps digging into my shoulders as I shuffled along.

Halfway to the rear of our convoy, the boss stopped, turning back towards our vehicle. Without asking why, I just followed him. My lungs were desperate for oxygen, needing it far more than I needed an explanation for the boss's decision to return to our vehicle.

I jumped back into the wagon, struggling to breathe.

'You okay, mucker?' Kev laughed.

I wanted to share the joke with him that I was in and out of our vehicle like a fucking yoyo, but it was still too hard to breathe, much less talk. Continuing to struggle for air, I took off my med pack and dropped it at my feet.

The interpreter taking cover in the back moved it away, placing it on the seat beside him.

'Thanks, Naveed,' I said quietly.

Our vehicle shunted forward as we hastily moved off.

Back on top cover, I cooled down, slowly recomposing myself. Kev was still laughing at my ordeal of running in the midday heat. Soldiers worldwide were all the same; I laughed at friends of mine getting beasted up and downs hills with a GPMG in Brecon. When it wasn't you on the receiving end, it was always funny.

We stopped near some open ground, and two company snipers set up on the roof of a compound nearby. 'Kingy', a young Jock from Stirling, was one of our snipers. These snipers were a godsend. Along with the Apache which just arrived on task, they set about tracking the Taliban of Marjah. The insurgents here weren't amateurs: they knew what they were doing and had just educated us in a textbook L-shaped ambush (from the left and the rear).

By this time, it was safe to attend to our casualty. The injured soldier was Chuckie, a tiny Scot, who was shot in the abdomen. LCpl Tom Rooke ('Rookey') has been taking care of him. Chuckie was the rear gunner manning the .50-cal. machine gun. His entry wound looked pretty high, so I was inclined to think that he might be in danger of developing a chest wound. No clinical signs as yet, but as a medic, it was my job to always think a few steps ahead. The nine-liner quickly went out, listing Chuckie as an urgent surgical cat-B. Our gunner needed a hasty evacuation.

Our company snipers, along with the Apache, were now even busier: they had to shield the casevac now under fire. Kev was busy on the net, and the rest of the company provided an all-round defence.

The Chinook came in swift and heavy. Attaching Chuckie's paperwork to his chest, I grabbed the first person that came off the rescue bird. I screamed all the important stuff in his ear, hoping that he heard my concerns about Chuckie's chest – his breathing rate had increased to a worrisome level, so my initial thoughts were correct. The MERT commander gave me the thumbs up before heading back up the ramp and into the helo. His force protection followed.

As the Chinook took off again, I looked around at the faces of our company. It was not such a great feeling being left in Marjah, knowing that we had to somehow get ourselves out of this shithole and back to Lashkar Gah.

We had the Apache escort us out of Marjah. There was sporadic small-arms fire, but nothing major. We made the desert leger unscathed and headed back to the MOB.

Kev and I were silent on the way back, with minimal chat and no banter.

As we got close to Lash, Kev said, 'You were right, mucker.'
'How so?'
'About us getting smashed,' Kev laughed.

I smiled grimly. Thirsty, I licked my lips, tasting the salt on the skin at the corners of my mouth. I had no energy left. The drive back had taken hours, and trying to stay alert as the sun was going down after such an eventful day had left me weary. Before heading back to my tent, I emptied a Lucozade rehydration sachet into my now boiling-hot bottle of water.

My recollection of Marjah has held my mind longer than I wished or intended, and I struggle to shake it off. Thinking about that time, though, I challenge anyone to tell me that women cannot handle being in combat or on the front line. We all share fear, and we all bleed the same. I would show Flashheart no mercy on the subject of women serving in frontline units. It takes a certain type, so go find them.

Sandbag chat over; back to the reality and the peace of PB Argyll. Resting on my bivvy, I catch a glimpse of Capt. Wood. He always finds ways to amuse himself, and now he is busy in his own little routine. I notice that he has the red iPod – that is, Flashheart's red iPod.

As I watch everyone going about their business, I almost forget to do my own chores.

I continue observing the company, amazed at the resilience of the young Jocks. They are surviving as best they can, just as we all are. I am drawn to the ordinarily common events that they make fun of. Someone only has to trip over in a gun position, or say something remotely feminine, for the place to erupt with laughter. They abuse each other all day long, but it's what gets them through the day. In fact, it's what gets all of us through. One minute, you might be the subject of ridicule, but if you are wounded the next minute, your section will carry you as many miles as necessary. Every man knows it. That's because when you get hurt, the lads get straight back to the serious business of being there for each other.

Capt. Wood is all over the fact that a much-needed injection of morale is required to motivate individuals carrying out the mundane tasks of equipment husbandry outside in the area housing the WMIKs. 'Sgt T,' he says with a smile, 'I think you may be developing a man-crush on Flashheart.'

Ham jumps on the bandwagon, adding, 'Aye, sir, that's why she keeps going on about him… she's after his other knee pad.'

Laughing, I shake my head. I realise I'm in a no-win situation, so I just go with it. 'Maybe I do have a man-crush on Flashheart. So what?' I try to keep my face stern, but one look at Ham has me giggling. 'You are a dick, Ham, but you are right about the knee pad.'

Cpl Ham McLaughlin is a driving force of antics around base; he finds comedy in everything. Even when he is pissed off, he can still manage to make a joke of something. He is constantly messing with people and their kit. If you fall on your arse when you go to sit down because your chair is suddenly missing from where it's always been, you can be sure that Ham has had something, or everything, to do with it.

Ham spends most of his time between the wall and the roof. He is another soldier suffering from the 'at war, ten years older' makeover. He constantly pesters me about what I know about when we are getting out of here. Ham was in Marjah with Kev and me, so we are all a tight-knit group

Everyone is still laughing because of the joke about my 'man-crush' on Flashheart, lifting morale for a moment. This is as it should be – soldiers never let the truth get in the way of a good lie. We all eagerly wait for another resupp. Information relayed over the net says that the mentoring team's medic is inbound. This is great news, because it means that I get Sean back. Afghan special ops are sending a team out with two British mentors. This is more good news, as they usually come with decent kit, and, moreover, better support.

Low on manpower, Davey needs a hand coordinating getting these guys off the helicopter and back to the base. I get my kit on, preparing myself for the trip out. Monty is taking a well-earned break, sleeping in the aid post. He and his men have been getting smashed these last few days. I am becoming more aware of just how much the boss achieves with this company, albeit not at full strength. Once every mission is complete, Maj. Clark ensures that there is a value-adding debrief: no bullshit, just anything that went well, and anything that could be done better.

When his men stand down, that's exactly what they get to do: relax. The boss leaves them alone. They respond by giving him total respect and 100 per cent effort at all times. These Jocks depend on each other, and they will die for one another without question. That's a rare commodity in this day and age, and I admire it.

I often chat with Monty about home and what he will do when he gets there. He is an old-fashioned family man who misses his wife and two daughters. He keeps a picture of his wife and girls beside his roll mat, just as Davey does.

Heading out to the HLZ, I catch up with Davey at the gate. He relays information that it is wheels up from Camp Bastion, so the helo will be arriving shortly. As we take up our positions I see that Davey is very close to where the bird normally sits when it lands. It's dark so his shadow is illuminated by the cylums. With the threat of attack on our helicopter so high, a short period of time on the ground is paramount. The coordination must be exact and smooth.

The Chinook lands heavy on the ground; large crates are dropped, followed by my medic and the guys mentoring the Afghan team. I grab hold of the first man and instruct him to follow me and stay close. Getting off a helicopter into an unknown area can be disorientating, and that's why I guide them in. The Chinook quickly lifts off as we make our way back into the PB.

Davey soon reveals that he was nearly squashed by the Chinook, reaffirming my earlier thought that he was way too close to where the bird normally sits. His team all get busy sorting through the stores, and Ham gets involved with the ATV and trailer stuff, still making time to mock Davey for his near-death experience, though.

I get back to the ops rooms with the new guys. As I take off my helmet, I see they seem shocked to be met by a woman. Quickly introducing myself in what now feels like an awkward first date, I hand them over to Maj. Clark. I take one of the mentors to where they will be housed along with their Afghan team. He asks me how long we have been here, and I give him the low-down of our time in Nad-e Ali thus far.

Making my way back to the ops room, I see that Davey is unpacking the stores, so I join the team and help out. It's been nearly three weeks, but our kit has finally arrived. Colleagues back in Lash have packed our bergens and sent them down to us.

I am excited that I will now have at least three pairs of socks and an equal amount of pants. I pull out a clean T-shirt that smells of washing powder; it reminds me of home. Planning to use the newly erected shower first thing in the morning, I leave a set of clean clothing at the top of my pack. Snuggling down in my bivvy bag, I look forward to tomorrow's shower and fresh clothes – what a treat. I am out of it within seconds and don't stir until first light. I've only slept for four hours, but it feels like longer.

The PB is alive this morning, with an extra spring in the step of every man. We are all so excited about the socks and pants. If I were anywhere else doing something different, these basic things wouldn't even cross my mind.

Out here, the sight of shower gel is like the discovery of the Holy Grail. My planned use of the shower is already on hold, though. A long line has formed, including the new arrivals. These two probably only showered six hours ago, and here they are wanting another one. I already know what unit they must derive from: shower-obsessed Royal Marines, no doubt.

Jen, Abbie, and I sit patiently outside the med room, waiting our turn. It crosses my mind that the shower cubicle is in open ground, next to the mortar line. The thought of taking a round while covered in soap suds suddenly decreases my desire to get in it. We busy ourselves making scoff and a quick brew. As I hand Abbie my ration pack, I notice one of our visitors has decided against having a shower and is now having a strip wash right in front of us. Like cavewomen, we all instinctively look at him. It is a genuinely funny moment. We all went into bloke mode, and the sight before us is far easier on the eye than Ferris's lily-white arse. Snapping quickly back into reality, I realise that my sausage and beans are far more important to me. It will take more than a six-pack to part me from my breakfast.

One by one, everyone gets some much-needed shower time, and it is definitely worth the wait. I am reluctant to wash my hair at first, as it has styled itself into a manageable bird's nest, but it has to be done. Scrubbed clean and with fresh clothing on, we wash our threadbare items; they are still serviceable, so no need to trash them.

Today, planning has started on upcoming operations that the company will mount on Taliban strongholds in Nad-e Ali. The boss is focused and has been given orders from command about key objectives that he must achieve. The area of Shin Kalay keeps appearing on the operations board. Shin Kalay is a Taliban haven, and brigade HQ wants us to patrol into the area to draw the Taliban out. The trouble is that the enemy knows the area far better than we do; the higher echelons are expecting a little too much from the troops on the ground. This type of patrolling is risky; our numbers are dwindling, so in my opinion, the gain does not outweigh the risk. The calculation seems disjointed.

Monty looks tired this morning. He and Lt Du Boulay have been commanding the fighting troops between them for days, even weeks now. Du Boulay borrows my single knee pad for most of his patrols; I suggest that, should the worst happen, Flashheart will have his second one at hand to give to anyone who requires it. Lt Du Boulay thanks me for the suggestion and moves off, with Abbie in tow. She is out this morning, so I say my 'stay safe' mantra and then get back into the medical room. Jen, Sean, and Gurung, our new OMLT medic, all are with me. Gurung was a part of our squadron back in Colchester, so it's great to have him back with us.

The patrol gets fifty metres out of Argyll before the rounds start pinging around the base. We are under attack, and it's come at a random time. This onslaught outside 'attack' hours catches the Afghans unawares.

It's not long before I hear the strained scream of 'medic!' Looking out from my cover, I see that one of the Afghan soldiers has been hit. The rest of his team carry him to the medical room; it is pointless pushing too many people out in the open, as we are still taking incoming.

The soldier wasn't wearing his body armour or helmet, and has taken a round through the upper chest. We drag him in and get to work. There is no exit wound. This means that the round must have travelled through some key organs, causing a fair amount of mess not visible to my anxious eyes.

Our systematic approach to casualties is what makes these situations work. A casualty in free fall requires quick interventions if life is to be sustained. Maybe a subclavian artery is clipped? We treat as we find, I want to make sure we do everything we can so I go through the detail of the MARCH-P process.

M – Initial diagnosis amounts to an internal bleed not visible to the eye. One entry, no exit wound. Sitting the casualty up alleviates any chest bleed at this point. Air rises and fluid falls, so if he is bleeding into the lung, it will pool at the bottom, allowing some chest movement. Chest seal in place occludes the entry hole. A decompression needle is on standby if and when it's required.

A – Quick insertion of a nasopharyngeal tube; the casualty tolerates it. Airway is open and clear. Jen maintains, with some assistance from oxygen, as I continue to run through possibilities.

R – Listening for breath sounds in a combat environment is not without its problems. Casualty stops breathing, and the side of injury is dull on percussion. Jen assists ventilations, and Gurung carries out needle decompression to injured side to buy us some time whilst we set about preparing an improvised chest drain. Further diagnosis indicates possible pneumohaemothorax, which is a mixture of air and blood, possibly trapped in the pleural space, with no chance to escape. This will result in compression of the heart and lungs, ultimately causing death via a complete mediastinal shift.

C – Major bleed; casualty is in hypovolaemic shock, and there is no radial pulse. In layman's terms, this means blood loss amounting to low blood volume. A team medic gains IV access; patient starts shutting down and goes into cardiac arrest.

CPR or cardio pulmonary resuscitation starts, and blood begins to push out of the decompression needle in the chest. Cardiac arrest in a patient through trauma is the worst-case scenario. His eyes are fixed, with pupils non-reactive. There is no palpable pulse, and with no defibrillator at point of wounding or in the aid post, manual CPR is continued.

Although hopeless, we crack on for the sake of the troops around us. Lt Col Nazim, the kandak commander, is with us throughout the ordeal, and the other Afghan soldiers are helping to pass kit and equipment to my medics.

The medical room is full of emotionally charged, armed Afghans. I take this into consideration as I decide to call time on our efforts to resuscitate the soldier. We do not have the luxury of an endless array of kit. I instruct Jen to stop the use of our only chest drain. Further use would achieve nothing; we could not turn off the tap inside the body, so the soldier has bled out internally.

With a lump in my throat, I tell my medics to stop. As a med team, we agree on this. I check for any signs of output, finally checking his pupils one last time. It's a bad moment for us all. Expressing my sympathy to the kandak commander and his men, I turn away. I update the boss, who in turn updates brigade HQ. They will call off the Chinook and MERT team and then wait for a suitable time to retrieve the soldier. His comrades don't wait around. They take his now-lifeless body away; they will wrap his body and pray for him, as is their tradition.

My medics look deflated, and it doesn't matter what uniform the soldier wore. His loss is shared by us all – it could have been any one of us lying there. We start the task of another clean-up. To be honest, I am getting sick of the sight and smell of blood. It has become too much of the norm. We sort through the medical kit quickly, and at the back of my mind, I know that the day is far from over.

With a patrol out on the ground, I move to the ops room to listen to their progress. From the net we soon learn that our call sign is already in trouble. The ICOM chatter reveals that the Taliban already has eyes on Du Boulay and his men. They continue to push forward, patrolling into an inevitable ambush. As crazy as it sounds, these are directives from higher command. They have air support which will allow enemy positions identified to be taken out, but it still doesn't explain the madness of patrolling into the kill zone of a determined enemy.

The 16 Air Assault Brigade is unlike anywhere that I have served before. Hard, fast, and aggressive is how they train, and, ultimately, how they fight.

'Contact wait out!' bellows across the net. At that moment, it's 'game on' again. The net is chaotic. Du Boulay is calling for CAS, and Capt. Wood is all over it; both Fast Air and Apache pilots are hungry for targets. Dangerously close to munitions being dropped, the platoon still hold their position. The Taliban stronghold is exactly that: as soon as they get eyes on the Apache they go to ground. As quick as they hide, they pop back up again, and now they are engaging our call sign from multiple firing positions. The firefight is relentless. Our 'not here' JTAC calls in fast air, and the sound of low-flying jets gets the nod of approval from everyone in our area.

The contact goes on for some time, so I start to plan for potential heat casualties. Two steps from the ops room door, I hear, 'Man down'; the words are repeated several times, and the news of a casualty shocks no one.

Capt. Wood turns to me. 'You all good, Channy?'

'Who is it, and where are they hit?' I say, asking Kev to message Monty when there is lull in the fighting.

Kev relays the answer as soon as he gets it. 'Boydy, gunshot wound to the thigh.'

The Taliban have the platoon pinned down one and a half clicks away. In this situation, a fighting withdrawal is the only option for Monty and his crew. Boydy (Pte Boyd) is a big lad who will need to be carried back to Argyll.

The firefight continues; even the Apache does not subdue the insurgents housed in Shin Kalay.

After what seems like a lifetime, I see the lads carrying Boydy; every man on the stretcher is in turmoil. We get hands on our casualty, and I am relieved to see he is still smiling. He's been shot straight through the shin, and the 7.62 mm round has come straight out the other side, embedding itself into the back of the thigh of the same leg.

With all my normal medical checks, I find no evidence to support that an artery was hit; Boydy's gotten lucky today. The other lads are in desperate need of water, as the heat has turned this casevac into a marathon. Guzzling water by the litre, Monty looks exhausted, and he's a fit soldier.

Boydy is surprisingly upbeat, and after assessment and treatment, he is stabilised. The only thing concerning him is a cigarette. In normal circumstances, I would hesitate, suggesting that he shouldn't have one. His vital signs are good, and he has responded well to treatment, so I decide to let Boydy have his cigarette. Right or wrong, I say yes; medical professionals the world over will probably frown upon it, but standing here in shitsville Nad-e Ali at this very moment, I choose not to be the medical 'cigarette police'. Boydy is a grown man who knows his own body, and his nerves are likely screaming for nicotine right now.

From a clinical perspective, Boydy's oxygen saturation is high, and he has a steady blood pressure. No tourniquet is required with the minimal blood loss he has sustained. He's doing well, all things considered. We prepare him for transportation, as the Chinook is inbound. Carrying him to the HLZ reaffirms what the guys have just faced getting him out of contact. Shots are fired at the incoming Chinook, and this sets the tone for the coming weeks. The RAF pilots aren't deterred – it would take more than a couple of rounds to stop them coming in to get us, of that I am sure.

As Boydy and our dead soldier are lifted, stories begin to emerge of the events that just passed. Monty tells me that Abbie carried the stretcher along with the blokes all the way back into Argyll. When I ask her about it she plays it down, joking about Boydy's weight. She's done herself proud and looks for no recognition for it. Abbie is the sort of medic that every commander wants: she doesn't moan, and she's able to hold her own amongst the platoon. I'm lucky to have her to rely on. Looking around at my medics, I know I'm lucky to have them all. Each one of them would perform above and beyond anything ever asked of them.

My attention shifts across the room as Monty collapses onto the floor. I learn that he fell into a ditch during the withdrawal, his face contorted with the pain. His body is now rigid, and he's unable to bend or move. By far the worst patient that I have to deal with, he is struggling to accept help and has no plans to make life easy for us. His lower back muscles have gone into spasm, caused by the fall itself or a combination of the fall and extraction under fire of Pte Boyd. Diazepam is my drug of choice this time, as it's an enabler that works wonders very quickly. The spasms stop, and Monty relaxes onto a stretcher. He'll be bedridden for at least two days.

The situation here is becoming truly unbearable. There are so many highs followed in quick succession by so many lows that it feels like one big fat test followed by another big fat test – and another and another.

For now, Monty is out of the game, and the boss asks me if we need to replace him. I learnt a fair amount from the physiotherapists that I've worked with in the past, so I tell the boss that I will work on Monty here in the PB.

'Thanks, Sgt T,' says Maj. Clark. He knows that Lt Du Boulay will have to take on the platoon alone; Cpl James Henderson will step up and assume Monty's role. Hendy is an experienced section commander, so he'll have no problem in taking up the slack for the platoon. Du Boulay is a quiet, unassuming officer; he has already proved his worth amongst his men, and they have warmed to him quickly. Tonight, he will move out for the first time without Monty.

A convoy coming from Lash will bring in some much-needed defensive stores, which will help fortify this small outpost ready for 3 Commando Brigade to take over. The convoy is travelling through the dark hours, a task which by now is fraught with danger. The force protection at Lash, made up of the remainder of B Company, will escort the convoy to the outskirts of Nad-e Ali, where they will be picked up by Lt Du Boulay and his men.

CHAPTER 6

PATROL BASE TEST

ICOM HAS STARTED PICKING UP STRANGE ACCENTS, indicating that foreign fighters are in our area. Intel soon identifies them as Pakistani and Chechen, which is a worrying development: these fighters will have travelled some distance to be here and will no doubt be very experienced in the killing fields, unlike the local farmers forced into battle by the Taliban. North of our location, a dead insurgent was found with an Aston Villa FC tattoo on his body; this worries us further, as fanatics of any religion are a danger to all societies, even if they are fans of our football.

Another Central Asian sunset comes and goes, and for some reason, there is no attack this evening. This is a welcome respite for the lads as they prepare to move out to meet the convoy. It's Jen's turn this time. I have gotten used to her working with me in the medical room. We have already dealt with our fair share of casualties, and our little team worked well. I could depend on Jen to take command if I were somewhere else on the base; after me, she is the most senior in our team.

As we settle in for the night, the familiar sounds of panic are heard over the net. Another shocker as the CLP heading into Nad-e Ali gets bumped by the Taliban. They were obviously waiting for them, hence the lack of incoming rounds on our base. The CLP now limps through the desert. It was like a 'welcome to the party', Taliban style. Instead of seeing smiling, welcoming faces or locals waving flags, guests were treated to the thuds of RPGs, followed by the rattle of the PKM or .50 calibre. If a VIP is inbound, then a 107 mm rocket will be offered up as a side to the shit pie so tenderly prepared by the sweet hands of the insurgency in Helmand – all going on against the backdrop of small-arms fire. It's like a never-ending musical score, but it wears thin after a while.

Dozing in the med room, I have learnt to sleep wherever and however I can. It won't be long before I am on my feet again, so I take rest whenever it presents itself. Moments later, we hear that our call sign has met up with the logistics patrol. The attack on them is more of a firepower display, and it hasn't created the number of casualties that the impressive sound would have you think. Timing has been on our side today. It looks like the Taliban didn't expect a road move. After all, what sort of lunatics would consider using an IED-littered road after dark? Oh, that's right, *we* are the very lunatics that did so.

The convoy arrives in the early hours of the morning. The lads, along with Jen, have been out all night. I jump up to give Davey a hand unloading the stores that have been sent. There are stacks of kit everywhere, as well as an overwhelming amount of ammunition. The crates are endless; someone in brigade HQ must have noticed that B Company might have moved up a couple of places on the priority board. Although the ammunition is welcome, it doesn't stop any of us from chuntering as the heavy boxes are unloaded. Worse still, they must be broken down into some sort of usage system: issuing amounts per man, per patrol, per day, and per week.

I haven't noticed until tonight just how stiff my body has become. Over a brew, I grimace at the stiffness while listening to the stories from the guys who have driven in with the supplies. They are from 13 Air Assault Regiment, Royal Logistics Corps (RLC). One soldier has been hit in the helmet by an RPG head which thankfully didn't detonate. One of the luckiest men on the planet, his dented helmet has since been placed in the archives of the Imperial War Museum.

The Jocks are happy once more: a morale box has been sent. The package includes cigarettes, cans of Pepsi, and Irn-Bru, a carbonated drink that is a basic requirement in any Jock diet. Although tired from the long day, the blokes finally have something to be chirpy about, and for a few hours it feels like Christmas has come early.

With the days starting to merge into weeks, PB Argyll slowly starts to develop into a bona fide outpost. More sandbags are filled to reinforce the gun positions on the roofs. That done, we fill our so-called larder. Our newly stocked rations are supplemented with tinned treats in the shape of pasta and vegetables. The Afghan soldiers make flatbread on earth-fired makeshift ovens; their bread is some of the best I've tasted. It provides the perfect accompaniment to the new ration pack main meal of chicken tikka masala. British army rations are divided up by letter, and my favourite is the pack marked F. It offers steak and vegetables most evenings, and adding a bit of curry powder or Tabasco sauce will offer up a decent scoff. The chicken tikka is from menu C, which is new and also has the best breakfast meal. Pork sausage and beans, it is the only breakfast that I can stomach; the rest are disgusting. Everyone on base gets up earlier than usual to try to get hands on menu C.

The fresh supplies of ammunition are now being distributed to the different corners of the base; the men of B Company have continued their risky strategy of patrolling into Shin Kalay, and now they have added Luis Barr, another Taliban stronghold.

Tonight we have more supplies coming in via Chinook. This lift is essential, as it carries the vital replenishment of drinking water. The water that we wash with comes via a black water container (jerry can). The Afghans have found a local water source that is good enough to wash with; thankfully, they also take on the responsibility of collecting it daily.

Logistically, everyone in the base works solidly together. Flashheart's Afghans are much more cohesive with him at the helm. He advises their commander, Lt Col Nazim, and so far he seems to achieve a fair amount with the small numbers that he has left. Flashheart continues to wear his two knee pads, just as some officers insist on wearing their sweat rags like cravats. It's almost a sign of his quirkiness: if he takes them off now, he will get ripped up by the blokes even more. If you are going to be different, it's best you stick with your chosen path. Meanwhile, the roads in and out of Nad-e Ali are getting worse. The convoy that delivered defensive stores just a few days ago gets hit hard on their way out. Several casualties are dealt with by our medical team back at Lash.

The Chinook drop will come in after midnight, so after last light the blokes prepare to patrol out to set up an outer cordon. This will at least stop anyone getting too close to the HLZ. Eagerly awaiting the resupp, Davey and his men prepare to deploy to the HLZ. Placing troops on the ground too early could potentially compromise the inbound Chinook and its crew. All seems well, which is usually never a good sign.

Sure enough, within seconds of the helo taking off from Camp Bastion, our interpreter, Naveed, sprints through to the ops room. Panicked, he says, 'Sir, sir, I hear the Taliban commander say that they will attack the helicopter tonight.'

'What the fuck!' Capt. Wood perfectly expresses exactly what we are all thinking.

The interpreter relays more. 'Through the ICOM I can hear a commander giving orders to a fighter who already has a full view of the landing site and its surrounding area. He is talking about a special fighter for the helicopter.' This is consistent with the Pakistan and Chechen accents from our intelligence source. Naveed continues, 'He is in position already, and they tell him to shoot the helicopter out of the sky.'

My throat is dry as I move next door to inform Davey and Monty about the story that is unfolding. Davey hurriedly gets the QRF together, as well as any other soldiers who are free. Sgt Maj. Tony Mason of the RI steps forward, volunteering himself and his men to assist the effort. In addition to the RI's task of mentoring the kandak, Tony has been working with Davey to man all of the outgoing 51 mm mortar missions. Tony has already earned the title as the calmest bloke in contact over the net, and his small team is a very welcome addition to the base – tonight more so than ever.

With no time to identify the firing point, the OC sends up all the intelligence gathered, hoping that brigade HQ will call off the Chinook until the morning. Undeterred, brigade staff weighs up the risk and deems it safe enough for our resupp to happen. I wonder what on earth we will do if the airframe is shot out of the sky: the fighting platoon is already out, and their cordon is covering the most-probable firing points. The kandak under the control of Flashheart has also deployed to cover more ground. That said, the enemy are set up somewhere with full eyes on the HLZ.

The boss turns to me, asking if we have the capability to deal with multiple casualties should the worst happen. I reassure him that we have set up other points outside of the CAP as casualty collection points (CCPs) so that I can triage correctly and prioritise our patients. We have stocked these points with the kit we have. Depending upon the severity of the injuries, we should be good; it isn't ideal, but it is what it is – and it's the best we can do. I have identified team medics within the company, and I mention that I might use these guys to man the other clearing station for less-serious injuries, if the tactical situation allows. Maj. Clark nods his head, looking as reassured as he can possibly be, considering the now-difficult circumstances.

The Apache gun ship arrives on station; it circles like a hawk searching for any dangers or signs of life visible only from the sky. Unfortunately, the Apache will have to be reactive this time, as a well-dug-in position will show no ground sign. A decent shooter will only reveal himself at the last safe moment. As the moment plays out, we can still hear the Taliban commander in direct communication with the insurgent who waits patiently in his hiding place.

Everyone's on edge, nerves frayed as we wait for our resupp to come in. We can only plan for so many scenarios; worrying about every possible eventuality will see you in an early grave, for sure. The plan is in place, so we roll with what we have – if you think about all of it too much, you will never lift your head from your pillow.

I deploy out to the HLZ with Davey, and we sit in the dark waiting for the sound of the Chinook engines. Out of nowhere, the airframe swoops in, hard and fast. The crew works like crazy to unload the water.

Fewer than twenty-three seconds down, the bird lifts with the shooter in position.

Immediately we hear the command, 'Fire now! Fire now!'

Suddenly, just as the Chinook is airborne, a bright streak

flashes through the darkness. A rocket has been fired. It flies straight past the window of the pilot's seat.

For a second I am numb, mouth breathing because I am unable to inhale enough air.

Tracer rounds from small arms almost instantly follow the rocket. The small-arms rounds look like tiny glow-in-the-dark insects or fireflies as they zip by.

The pilot shunts the huge airframe forward nervously. Its huge engines soar as the bird lifts. The Chinook narrowly escapes another rocket before flying off into the darkness.

On the ground, the sound of some muffled 'woo hoos' carry through the empty night air.

'Thank fuck for that Ham. Let's get this shite back in!' Davey shouts.

When we return to the ops room, the boss and Capt. Wood are sitting at the desk, chuckling. It turns out the Taliban commander has ordered the execution of the special shooter who missed his target, the helo.

Naveed translates the commander's last radio transmission. The insurgents still use medieval, sometimes barbaric means to achieve their aim. Stories of how the mujahideen treated captured Russian officers were every man's worst nightmare.

Just as the subject crops up, as if by magic, Flashheart appears in the doorway. Capt. Wood tells him that if he is taken with elements of the kandak he will be sodomised by his captors. Looking hesitantly around the room, Flash smirks and then adds, 'That won't be happening any time soon, people.'

Back to my bed space in quick time and positive that my roll mat is getting thinner by the day, I place my weapon down by the side of my bivvy bag. The OMLT had the sense to bring camp cots with them, but the rest of us continue to sleep rough on the floor.

Laying my head for a couple of hours, I wake only for my death stag on the radio. After last night's incident, I will patrol into the district centre of Nad-e Ali with the boss tomorrow. We must identify a secondary HLZ, large enough for our Chinooks to land and manoeuvre safely.

I am glad to escape the PB for a couple of hours. I do understand my position here – Maj. Clark needs medical information at a moment's notice, and with no doctor, that leaves me to do it, which means I am stuck in the confines of the PB. Our base is small, so a short trip away is most welcome. The size of the PB creates other problems too: the Taliban need only fire in our general direction to know they will hit something. This is worrisome indeed and constantly in the back of all of our minds. Perhaps a short trip will clear my head, helping me to stop waiting for the next attack. Nevertheless, events in Marjah taught me to be very careful what I wish for: I was initially excited about that foray too.

Plus, we have lately been fighting in places where historical sites still stand. Places of worship or the run-down ruins of what were once great forts, these sites are sacred to the indigenous population but fraught with danger for non-natives of the region. This brings us into 'military tourism' to a certain extent. I have developed a distinct dislike for the military tourists of the world. Military tourism is usually undertaken by the civilian element of government-backed projects, and my dim view on the combat tourist came about through witnessing civilians in flowing flowery skirts wearing unsuitable strappy sandals deploying out on trips to the Qala-e-Bost Arch on the outskirts of the provincial capital (Lash). This eleventh-century arch marks the primary route into what was the ancient military citadel town of Bost. The visits to the arch served no tactical or reconstructive purpose, but they did create the perfect combat tourist photo opportunity. This 'tourism' has become a pet peeve of mine, as well as another subject that I have become all too ready to voice my opinion on. This is not without reason: it's usually the resident infantry company that provides the outer security cordon for these little jaunts. Personnel of any description should never be deployed on the ground unless there is a specific tactical purpose or mission; I include hearts and minds in those missions.

These thoughts flit through my mind while I consider the prevailing logistics of our PB. The situation on the roads around Nad-e Ali is making any potential road moves out of here impossible. I realise that movement by air and under the cover of darkness is the only plausible way that B Company will get back to 'Lash Vegas'. That 107 mm rocket got very close, and the Taliban's ability to buy surface to air missiles (SAMs) is a reality that makes this move far from attractive.

As normal routine presses on, non-battle injury and sickness have become prevalent, and this has started to deplete our numbers with the same gusto as our enemy is doing. Diarrhoea of some sort is presenting itself in everyone; and this is often accompanied by dehydration and fatigue.

Foot problems are the most crippling, as the blokes' boots are sodden with water. Using the irrigation channels as cover during contact means that many of the platoon are knee-deep in water while fighting. Insect bites are becoming infected, and the list of maladies goes on and on. Suffice to say that my sick parade is growing on a daily basis.

I make an off-the-cuff remark to one of the section's 2IC about the possibility of swapping the Jocks on the wall and roof gun teams with soldiers in the fighting platoon. This will offer the guys suffering most some much-needed rest. Every man is working as hard as the next, just in different ways.

My suggestion gets back to Monty, who's not best pleased. I overhear him griping the section 2IC for mentioning it. In hindsight, I wish that I mentioned it directly to Monty in private; however, my regret quickly turns to anger when I hear Monty brief one of his blokes up for coming sick. I hear him further explain that the guys must see him prior to coming to see me in the aid post.

'Tell me that I didn't just hear that,' I say to a stunned Abbie. Jumping up off my seat, I fly through to my medical room where Monty is resting.

The situation is not unlike the times when I would argue with my brothers as a kid, and I hope it doesn't end the same way that they often would: with me stabbed in the temple with a fork or choked out for twenty seconds or so in the passageway. At home, being the youngest of five was a dangerous job – especially if you had a smart mouth like mine.

Now I confront Monty as I walk through the door. He rightfully defends the command of his platoon, just as I defend my suggestion to alleviate the fact that the blokes were in shit state. With two strong characters like Monty and me, it's never going to be a smooth ride.

As always, I am the first to get my point across. 'Be sure to let me know if any fucker needs my help when they're bleeding out, Monty. Or are you going take control of our wounded from your fuckin' pit space, along with your own bad back?'

'Fuck off, and get yourself te fuck, Channy,' Monty angrily replies.

As I've said, Monty and I aren't dissimilar in character, which makes for an interesting ten minutes. B Company relies heavily on us both, and the pressure is starting to show. Davey walks into the room, looks at us, shakes his head, and walks straight back out. It's clear that he is disappointed to see Monty and me squabbling like two private soldiers.

I head out of the CAP, still angry. Nothing has been resolved. Everyone heard the fracas, but no one got involved, and no one says anything.

Slumping down onto my roll mat now, I remember a conversation that Monty and I had no more than a week ago. It was the same day that we lost one of the kandak soldiers. Monty came into the CAP, only to find the place covered in blood and me up to my neck in shit. He had been out on patrol when the incident happened, so he missed most of it. I made the decision to stop my team's work on the Afghan soldier after we had exhausted much of our already depleted medical kit.

When Monty arrived, he asked me at what point I would decide to stop working on him or one of his men. He wanted to know how much time we would spend exhausting ourselves. Realising that it was something that I hadn't even thought about, I explained to him that although we weren't kitted out as well as Lash, as a team we would keep going until they were on the helicopter. I truly meant what I said: for the sake of morale, both our own and that of the troops left behind, we would keep going. Clearly, though, if half a body or a head is missing, the unenviable decision is made for you.

Bearing all this in mind, I walk back into the medical room. I look at Monty, knowing that we are in this together. He knows that, as medics, we will go as far as we can for him and his men; I know that they regard us as their own.

I look at Monty now, trying my best to stay semi-serious. We both start laughing.

'Sorry, mate,' Monty says.

'It's my fault,' I reply. 'I didn't mean anything by it. I just made a passing comment, that's all.'

We are a solid team, and everything is running smoothly. Supporting each other in everything is a must. I rely heavily on Monty to keep my medics safe out on the ground, and he relies on me to keep his men alive and healthy.

The only good to come out of the argument is that we both blow off a fair amount of steam. Our argument has emptied the aid post, and I am glad that no one else chose to get involved. When you are attached to the infantry, it's very easy to turn up and make up the numbers, but my regiment didn't deploy medics like that. When numbers are so small, every soldier must add value to any given situation.

Understanding tactics, both good and bad, and understanding where you as an individual fit in the group setting is crucial. We are trained to add value. Being the expert in my field, I have to make sure that I never lose control of my own mission.

In this instance, Monty and I are both right; our miscommunication has just confused things, as miscommunications always do. It's like when you send a text or email, and you hit 'send' before explaining exactly what you mean. When you read it back to yourself, you realise that you sound like one of the crazies off that TV show *Jeremy Kyle*, but it's too late: the message is out there, and whoever you've sent it to is already reading it.

Half an hour passes, and all is forgotten. All is well between Monty and me. I am sure of this because, much to my disgust, Michael Buble is back haunting my speakers.

Our biggest test is yet to come, and none of us has the luxury of foresight. My bivvy is calling, and I am ready for sleep. The night zips by, and morning sees our call sign prepare to move out to find the possible secondary HLZ.

As I exchange banter with Flashheart about his dual knee pad action, I retrieve my own knee pad from 2Lt Du Boulay.

Flashheart's character lends itself to life in a PB. He has inspired a new test that I will perform on potential new friends – or my future husband – the PB test. I sell the idea to Capt. Wood, who takes it on as his own. The test is one question followed by a yes or no answer; you can wean out the idiots, saving time and sometimes money.

The question is simply this: would I as an individual spend any length of time with him or her in a small isolated PB? Flashheart manages to scrape by the reasoning; firstly by his double knee pads, and, more importantly, because of his red iPod. Character goes a long way in the military: those who have it tend to succeed wherever they go.

As we deploy out of PB Argyll, the men of B Company seem to have found their second wind. Jokes are shared and the blokes berate each other as the patrol steps off. It's amazing what a day's rest can do for morale. We patrol through the district centre, making our way past the police station that housed us that first night.

Not wanting to miss an opportunity to mock, Kev reminds me of my resourceful spooning of our interpreter to keep warm on the roof.

'Good one, Kev,' young Ferris says, applauding Kev's vigilance. We all laugh.

It's hard to believe that we were ever here. That night seems a world away... so much has happened since then.

As we approach the open space, it appears large enough to manoeuvre a Chinook. I soon notice that there is not a person or dog in sight. Nad-e Ali is completely deserted.

Discarded drug paraphernalia is strewn around the ground where I am about to steady my knee, and I am very thankful for my knee pad. Maybe this warrants Flashheart's two! With used needles all over the ground around us, I warn the guys behind me to be careful with the placement of their hands.

We settle down in all-round defence as the boss and Davey get busy marking grids and taking photos. We don't hang about: the trip back to Argyll is quicker than the trip out. Upon our return, the Afghan special ops team and their mentors are busy preparing to patrol out for the first time. The boss orders the PB to stand to, acting as a QRF for the Afghans and their mentors.

The small group deploys out, heading south. Within ten minutes, their patrol gets whacked. 'Contact, wait out!' booms across the net. As the firefight gathers pace, we can hear worrying dialogue over the net. The shouting of the Afghans drowns out British accents. Our interpreter tries to relay but can't make out the entire conversation; he mentions that two of the Afghan team may have turned their weapons on the entire patrol, including the two British soldiers.

'What the fuck?!' Davey looks at the boss, his face reddening with anger.

A British voice comes over the net, and we hear it clearly this time. 'Topaz zero alpha, returning to your location now with two hostile prisoners. Out.'

A crowd gathers as the soldiers return to the PB. The two detainees have been disarmed, and their Afghan comrades drag them in. The team look dishevelled and shocked by the drama that has unfolded. The Brit mentors choose to house the two in the back of separate snatch vehicles. The boss is quickly debriefed about the intent of our guests. Although operating independently on the ground, the team still came under the charge of Maj. Clark when housed in the PB. With nowhere else to secure the two prisoners, the snatch Land Rovers are backed up to the outside wall of the aid station; that way, we can keep an eye on them medically. They have plenty of ventilation and water – albeit in a confined space, perhaps a little too much ventilation, as we would later discover.

So the story unfolds that during the initial stages of the ambush, the two sympathisers turned their weapons on the entire team. A struggle ensued, and, thankfully, they were overpowered by the rest of the patrol.

Later in the day, one of the mentors asks if I will check on one of the prisoners who sustained injuries during the initial struggle.

'No worries,' I say. 'I will just grab my kit.' I climb up onto the roof of the vehicle so I can get eyes on through the hatch at the top.

The mentor opens the hatch and peers in, and I notice a look of shock on his face. 'Gen, gen, gen, no fucking way!' he says, sounding completely puzzled.

For a moment, I am inclined to think that the prisoner has somehow died. But then, as I take a look myself, I see that the back of the vehicle is empty – the prisoner is missing! While I take in the magnitude of what this means, I notice my yellow sharps container still sitting in its position on the side of the vehicle. So a member of Afghan special ops, who is also a Taliban sympathiser, is on the loose in the base, but everything is okay because my multipurpose yellow sharps bucket is still intact. The things that I think about at times are often hard to comprehend.

All positions around the base are informed, and everyone goes into a state of heightened alert. Every man has his weapon closer than before, and movement is kept to a minimum. Any complacency that may have crept in has diminished. Once informed, the kandak commander goes ballistic, demanding that his men seek out the soldier who gave the escapee help with the breakout.

The tension between the Afghans and Jocks is creating an atmosphere of suspicion and mistrust. The base is supposed to be a safe haven for us all – well, as safe as it gets in Nad-e Ali. The escapee is more than likely armed with intent to kill; he will wreak havoc in the camp. A manhunt is under way, and no stone is left unturned; every inch of PB Argyll is covered.

An hour goes by before an Afghan soldier is found harbouring the escapee. The rapid response from Lt Col Nazim and his men leave no doubt as to where their loyalties lie. The prisoner is found and dealt with in a fashion that is not acceptable in our military. Fortunately for him, they hand him over to us, so he is lucky this time.

I check him over to confirm that he is okay. Looking into his eyes, I notice a glazed, almost vacant gaze. It's like he can see me but doesn't want to see me; he is shaking and breathing heavily. I have never seen this before: he's alive physically but lifeless in his soul. He makes me feel numb. Pausing for a moment, I ask our interpreter to tell the soldier that everything will be okay. I give him some water while I check for signs of torture. The Afghans have thrown him about a bit; nothing major, though.

If we want to become too interested in their personal conduct, we might do well to start looking at the treatment given to the dancing (or 'chai') boys that they keep. It's tradition in Afghanistan for the men of the house to keep boys as sex slaves, and I have seen many on our travels. It is a cultural thing that I have no desire to accept or understand.

In the past few years, there have been several incidents in which Afghan soldiers have turned on British and American troops. Thankfully, the bond between the ANA and the coalition is growing in the main, and the plan to train more Afghans is ever developing.

Orders come from higher command that the whole Afghan

special ops team is to be extracted; they will move later tonight and won't be replaced.

The rest of the day is relatively quiet, but fresh reports about future Taliban intentions keep the chatter alive in the ops room. They are desperate to bring down one of our helicopters, and ICOM reveals that they will target the next resupp. Working out that our moves by road have all but ceased, they are quick to change their tactics.

Davey plans to stretch the outer cordon further; our helicopters won't stop coming, so the threat is always looming. The extraction of the mentors and their team goes by without incident.

A night of unbroken sleep looms, so I put my iPod in, and off I go. I awake at first light, refreshed. Stand-to follows, and then, with my morning routine over, I make use of some quiet time. Taking my turn on the satellite phone, I call home.

'Hello?' Mum answers.

'Hi, Mum, it's me... just checking in.'

'Everything okay?' she asks in her soft Scottish accent.

'All good, Mum, just counting down the days here.' I don't tell her where I am or what I am doing. Sitting on the tailgate of one of the WMIKs guarding the corner, it's a relief just to hear her voice.

Young Jock Gaz Wilson is manning the .50 calibre on top of the WMIK. Gaz is a junior soldier. He had a tough time growing up, losing his mum at a young age. What amazes me is his lack of bitterness; he lives life to the full and embraces everything. He cares for his younger brother and tries to do best by him. Soldiers like Gaz make me miss home, and I am always grateful for the family that I have.

Gaz observes a group of fighting-age males and relays the information to Scotty Pew on the roof.

I get to my third or fourth sentence before the .50 calibre lets rip above me. Very much aware that my mum is on the other end of the line, I say, 'Love you, Mum,' and then hang up in haste.

'For fuck's sake!' I yell as I scramble into cover before making the mad dash along the wall receiving incoming – I have to get to my body armour and helmet. The rattle from the huge gun is deafening; it makes my teeth chatter.

I wish that I'd chosen a different moment to call home. God only knows what my mum must be thinking. But this is how it is. You are forced to try to create a normal routine in the prevailing environment. Situations can go from nothing to everything in seconds, so you make the call home whenever you can.

Scotty Pew confirms six kills, and it looks like they were setting up for an attack on us later, moving mortar rounds before randomly engaging Gaz Wilson's position.

Morale is dented amongst the soldiers of PB Argyll: the makeshift shower has taken a 7.62 mm round at head height, so everyone is to revert back to being feral – no washing again. Mega!

I am desperate to call home to alleviate any fears that my mum may have had, but when I call all is well. I don't think that she understood what all the noise meant, so I don't tell her; my family would have to wait for me to write a book in order to find out what I had been up to in Afghanistan.

CHAPTER 7

Mass Casualties

THE ARRIVAL OF THE THROATCUTTER CALL SIGN INTERRUPTS the peace that morning habitually brings. The boss welcomes the news that the turbine move to Kajaki is complete, as it brings all lead elements to the CP for a much-needed reorg. Planning will become more focused in light of the success. Everyone's favourite 'big picture' is looking just peachy, and a switch in the brigade's main effort means that the priority is now the handover of all areas of operation to 3 Commando Brigade.

Maj. Clark, along with 2IC Capt. Wood, is busy devising plans for offensive operations tomorrow. With areas surrounding Nad-e Ali becoming increasingly unstable, 16 Brigade has deployed the PF platoon to operate in and around Marjah to our south. Small groups of Afghan special ops teams are patrolling the desert to our north. The kandak's main effort is to push into the areas proving to be the most problematic. In recent weeks, Shin Kalay and Luis Barr have been highlighted as insurgent strongholds.

Monty is back in action so he, under the command of 2Lt Du Boulay, will reinforce the Afghans should the need arise. The fighting platoon will conduct low-level ops just over a click away from the PB. Monty's mood is light this morning; he is far happier back with his men and not stretcher-ridden in the aid post. The Throatcutters will assume the role of a roving quick reaction force; they will satellite the area and be on hand to provide mutual support to our fighting patrols and/or to serve as a casualty extraction team along with us. These are going to be significant and dangerous operations that will see us through to our end of tour. Suffice to say that 3 Commando Brigade can't get here quick enough.

I detect through levels of banter that the soldiers of B Company are more resolute than ever. This tour has already claimed the life of one member of the regiment. He was killed by a legacy mine left here by the Russians, and every man of the company is still grieving his loss. (His family, still very much grief-stricken, do not want his name mentioned. I respect their wishes and fully understand the devastation of losing a loved one.)

The thought of going home has motivated the Jocks to finish their very personal battle to hold Nad-e Ali. Every step invested in this mission has safeguarded the ground, making sure that the district has not fallen to the Taliban. This AO is our main effort, and every soldier is committed to the mission. Despite our loss, we shall persevere.

Flashheart prepares for his big day out, engaging in his now-customary process: his knee pads are pre-positioned, fresh coffee has been pressed, and Marlboro Lights are at the ready. His hair is more bouffant than normal as he pops into the CP for a quick shit chat prior to his departure. I have grown fond of his once-irksome character. Flash doesn't take life too seriously, and he has the ability to laugh at himself. He is genuine and kind-hearted. I will probably read about him one day for having just won a Victoria Cross or something equally outrageous. Needless to say, the kandak is more than happy to follow Flashheart into battle.

Sgt Maj. Tony Mason of the RI will deploy alongside the kandak, medic Gurung is assigned to the mentoring team, and Sean will deploy with Monty and his crew. I'll keep Abbie and Jen with me. We prepare our medical room as we normally would, and then we see Sean and Gurung off as they leave camp.

The moment both patrols deploy, a dicker (or spotter) is located through binoculars by Scotty Pew on the roof. A spotter will often be the eyes for waiting insurgents prior to any type of attack or ambush. A good dicker is one that is not seen. This one must have learnt his craft at the school of arse-clownery; he must have been skiving off or asleep during the covert dicker/spotter lesson. Unarmed, the male is noted and followed until he disappears into the thick vegetation that surrounded him.

The mass exodus of blokes allows me to tend to the small number of troops left in Argyll. I keep busy administering basic physiotherapy techniques on the increasing number of non-battle injuries in the PB. Abbie is first in, complaining of uncomfortable lower back pain.

I set about the muscles on either side of the lower spine, and Abbie winces in pain as the gristly knots come into contact with bone. We listen to music through the small set of speakers on the old wooden desk, and I start to relax, but I am doubtful that the soothing tones are helping Abbie to do the same. Coldplay's 'Fix You' sets the tone for what is to become the single worst day in Nad-e Ali – for me, anyway.

The sound of small arms ignites the radio net into action, followed by the thunderous roar of DShKs. The eruption of firepower is ear-splitting.

Scotty Pew has full view of the surrounding area from the gun position on the roof, and it appears that the kandak are being engaged. Capt. Wood and the JTAC get busy calling for CAS in the shape of the Ugly call sign, and it doesn't take long for help to arrive. As the Apache gunships circle the sky above, Monty's crew are holed up in a small compound; they will sit tight until the full picture emerges. The latest information warns of imminent attacks on both call signs: insurgents have pinpointed Monty's position, and ICOM chatter confirms that the Taliban know which compound and how many men are on task.

The Afghan kandak caught up in close-quarter fighting are engaging enemy at will. CAS waits for confirmation from the JTAC to neutralise targets. The sound of the hellfire missile from the Apache silences the guns for a split second; at that moment, there is not a better sound anywhere on earth. The hellfire is an air to surface missile (ASM). With the Apache having the ability to carry sixteen of the bad boys, all is well – or so we think!

The kandak's glory is short-lived. Radio traffic soon comes to a grinding halt. Abbie, Jen, and I are in the middle of a conversation which comes to an abrupt end, as a panicked voice comes over the net, the stifled words 'mass casualty' barely audible. A long silence follows.

The strangled cry repeats three more times: 'Mass casualty! Mass casualty! Mass casualty!' This wasn't the calm Tony Mason that I was accustomed to.

Abbie bolts upright, Jen looks at me, and I look at the floor, holding my head in my hands and trying to make sense of what I just heard. Taking a deep breath, I head through to Maj. Clark. My pulse increases, and those sweaty palms are back.

Capt. Wood calls the Apache off just before it goes in for its second run. The boss and 2IC are wearing the same cold and clammy look that I am.

As soon as I start to speak, I notice that my mouth has dried up. 'What's happened?' I ask, all but choking on the words.

In an exhausted but calm voice, Maj. Clark explains, 'We have an incident involving the kandak and OMLT.'

Tony's voice comes back over the net. 'Topaz zero alpha, ten casualties; most of my team have been hit, including my med call sign.'

The CP is silenced; it's the pause that every commander has prior to making a workable plan. Head in hands, focusing on what needs to be done, this way of thinking is what makes the military the best in a crisis. There will be no running around like headless chickens. It's times like this that all the training and preparation for deployment shows its value. No shouting or foaming at the mouth, this is what controlled panic looks like. You might be at 30,000 feet and rising on the inside, but on the outside you remain stalwart and typically British. I focus on my own mass casualty plan, and of course I have one. Will it work? Only time will tell. The annoying but very true saying of 'no plan survives the first contact with the enemy' irritates me when I think about it. I take a few deep breaths – not big obvious sighs, just enough to ensure that my brain is receiving oxygen – and then I set about the task at hand. I reassure the boss that we will square the situation away with the medics that we have before moving next door to prepare for our inbound casualties.

I gather the two team medics of 5 Scots: LCpl Aaron Wells ('Wellsee') and Pte Farrel Foy. These guys can deal with our walking wounded or less needy, and I set them up in an area just outside the aid post. Jen and Abbie will take on the more-serious casualties, and I will oversee the effort, making interventions if required. Medical scene control is as important as treatment itself: if you get it wrong, the situation free-falls, as do the patients. We have set up separate CCPs to house our wounded.

Meanwhile, the Throatcutters move rapidly to the kandak's position; their task is to get our men back to the PB so that we can treat them. The boss orders Monty's platoon to finish on task and assist the stricken call sign by providing an all-round defence for them. Things are looking good. Ever optimistic, I wonder if, for the first time ever in history, a plan will survive the annoying 'first contact' scenario.

Like a reliable old Casio watch, the well-thought-out plan survives less than five minutes.

'Man down... Man down!' Monty screams over the net.

As soon as they left the compound, the Taliban opened fire. The enemy patiently observed as the platoon conducted low-level ops in and around selected compounds. One of the lads has taken a round straight through the femur. A complicated injury at the best of times, this is news that we could do without.

'What the fuck is happening?' I say to Abbie.

My brain is working overtime, and Monty is now pinned down in the compound that they occupied initially. I put those guys to the back of my mind. Our priority is to deal with what's coming through the door. Sean will be working hard if the femoral artery is hit, but he is more than capable. I gather my medics and brief them on our plan of action; this is the calmest that I have ever seen them. It's a good feeling for me as commander that there aren't any doubts in our team.

Sean is taking care of business, and news from the mentoring team indicates that Gurung is still managing to treat the other injured soldiers in his crew. It's time to put my plan in action. Grabbing anyone who is free in the PB, I tell them I need help carrying stretchers. It's no surprise that I am not short of volunteers. Once again up from rest periods, the PB braces itself.

Brigade HQ back in Lash has started screaming for details of casualties. The boss wants quick and accurate information in order to guarantee the best possible outcome for our injured. One Afghan soldier is confirmed KIA on the ground, and then the first casualties start to arrive.

With casualties strewn across the tailgates of vehicles, it's messy. Quick checks tell me we have two cat-Bs so far (plus one KIA). One by one, I triage and assign our wounded. As I work my way through, all the years of training kick in. The head injury to Jen, and the open chest wound to Abbie. The more serious are taken straight through to the CAP. We quickly receive more casualties: four cat-Cs. Wellsee and Foy set about patching them up as best they can.

The mentoring team are all back in Argyll now, with several wounded. Gurung continues to treat, ignoring the shrapnel in his own legs. I order him to stop so he can receive treatment himself. I've never been a fan of pulling rank, but he is starting to look a little pasty. Gurung isn't the only one of the mentoring team wounded: Tony Mason has fragmentation damage to his arms.

Flashheart has somehow managed to escape unscathed. Just the sight of him gives me a much-needed morale boost. He is in shit state, and his hair and kit are more dishevelled than ever. The wide-eyed panic in his face is back, so I am laughing at the very sight of him.

'You okay, sir?' I ask.

Struggling to breathe, he replies, 'All good, Sgt T.' Once again, he adds value at the most-inappropriate time.

I count up the casualties we have so far: eleven wounded, and one man KIA. Monty has yet to bring in his cat-B, which will make twelve. The boss wants a casualty report, and quick: the MERT are waiting to deploy from Camp Bastion, and brigade HQ is sending two Chinooks for the lift. So I systematically reassess all of our casualties: tourniquets are in place, airways are stable, breathing rates are acceptable, the all-important radial pulses are palpable, and the splints look good. I am happy that we have done all that we can. Our wounded are now stable enough to handover. I confirm with the boss that we as a team are good to go. Monty will meet us at the HLZ, bringing his casualty there to save time.

The intense overpowering midday sun makes for an interesting pre-lift casualty brief to our stretcher bearers. Wiping sweat from my eyes, I wait for confirmation that both helos are airborne from Camp Bastion. With no time to waste and with everything under control, we begin to move our injured towards the HLZ.

I spot an overzealous Afghan soldier driving his truck at speed in the direction that we were now heading. It looks like he may be trying to assist, but his reckless headless-chicken reaction is dangerous; this sort of lunacy will only create more casualties. So back to the start it is for me: scene control. Smashing the butt of my rifle onto his windscreen, I signal for him to stop. Trying to remain calm, I demand, 'What the fuck are you doing?' I force my fully armoured frame into his open driver's window, removing the keys from the ignition. Abbie would later laugh that from her view near the CP she could see me hanging halfway out his window, like a great white hanging out of a shark dive cage, apparently. By this point, I reach for the hand brake, gripping the keys and his collar tightly in my other hand. I wait for the other Afghan soldiers assisting me to sort the soldier out. They drag him from his vehicle before moving him away.

Staying on task, I call vehicles forward. They are laden with our wounded, and the stretcher bearers follow on foot behind the vehicles. The scene we face takes my breath away: splashes of vibrant red cover the desert camouflage shredded by the blasts, barely covering the bodies of our wounded. People are talking to me; I see their mouths moving, but I can't hear anything. We have casualties that are physically hurt, but we also have young men in precarious mental states. Making ground slowly, we edge towards the HLZ. I give Abbie one set of handover notes, and I take the other. The four cat-B patients are split. The remaining cat-Cs will be divided equally between the airframes.

Sean and Monty suddenly appear at the front gate, with the femur fracture and Pte Coakse ('Coaksee'). The femur has been very well splinted, in light of where they were during point of wounding; he has been extracted, much to the detriment of the call sign. Another fighting withdrawal has created a heat casualty. Coaksee's eyes are rolling in the back of his head, and he is barely conscious. I can't risk keeping him here, so he gets evacuated along with the rest.

Sean tries to administer fluids orally while the rescue birds hover above, but there's no cover to site an IV. Time just isn't on our side. The information has already been logged, so I will have to make sure that the MERT don't miss Coaksee or overlook him. There are no stretchers left, so Sean will carry Coaksee onto the helo.

We settle the casualties down in the usual position to the side of the landing site, and without warning, one of the Afghan soldiers decides to walk straight across the HLZ. Two Chinooks are hovering above him, coming in to land. By some miracle, the downdraught has disorientated him enough to move him towards my position. I grab him by the scruff of the neck before forcing him face first into the dirt, all the while nursing the vision of him losing his head to the low rotor blades at the front of the Chinook.

The airframes land simultaneously; the familiar faces on the back of the airframes are a welcome sight. Doctors from my regiment hand us bags full of medical kit and all the good stuff from the store housed in Camp Bastion.

The casualties go on, and my Afghan medical team get it right this time: they control themselves, and for a moment, I am proud of them. I explain Coaksee's situation to the receiving team, and they are all over it. As casualties are systematically handed over, our team move off and take cover from the downdraught.

The two Chinooks lift off the ground together. It's incredible, and the buzz from adrenaline is like nothing that I have felt before. As the dust settles, the sound of the engines peters out into the distance. I have a weird moment, wishing that I was on one of those birds, heading home. Running back to the PB, I don't dwell on my 'moment' too much, pretty sure most people are feeling the same.

The aid post is in chaos; I don't know where to start. Blood coats much of our equipment, and the sodden clothing from casualties, including their shoes, are still in place where their bodies once lay. Vomit covers the floor where Jen dealt with the head injury. Of all our patients, I was most doubtful of his recovery. Grabbing a pack of water bottles, I pass them around the team. Nobody speaks for ten minutes or so, silently taking in the magnitude of what has just happened. Fiddling with a clinical waste bag, I forget for a second why I have the damn thing in my hand.

Our solemn mood changes to an angry one as stories emerge about the cause of the carnage today. Our guys weren't shot up by a well-dug-in Taliban position, nor did they encounter a daisy chain of IEDs, as initially thought. They were hit by the hellfire missile from the Apache gunship (or fragmentation from it) – the same hellfire that we had celebrated hours earlier. No one took the news calmly, least of all Davey and the boss.

After a tense regroup in the CP with all call signs in attendance, it transpires that friendly grids given over the net have been miscommunicated as enemy grids. The Apache pilot wasn't at fault; he engaged what he thought were enemy positions. Luckily, Capt. Wood called the Apache off just before he was going in for a second run. The 2IC's quick reaction stopped the Apache from re-engaging.

No one wants to take responsibility for such a colossal fuck-up. The patrol commanders thrash it out in the ops room, leaving relations between B Company and the Throatcutters strained, to say the least. No one is talking, and I see that my command chain is in no hurry to kiss and make up. The truth is that the situation happened during a phase of fighting commonly known as the 'fog of war'; it's never welcome, but it happens, and in some cases it is unavoidable.

Our base is on its knees, when it comes to manpower; we need battlefield replacements. Looking around, we as a group are threadbare. My own positive mental attitude is waning. Sgt Maj. Tony Mason from the mentoring team is out of the game, and Davey needs a number two for outgoing 51 mm mortar missions. I offer my assistance, and he accepts. Times have become desperate, and it's very much a case of each of us doing whatever we are capable of doing to help hold Nad-e Ali.

The military's Law of Armed Conflict states that as a combat medic, I can only fire in anger to protect myself and/or my casualties, unless the circumstances are deemed exceptional. With sixty-six out of one hundred men injured and four Afghan soldiers dead, I am comfortable with the notion that Nad-e Ali is now in exceptional circumstances. I don't take the decision lightly, but I think about us overrun and slaughtered by the Taliban. I can see the spun headline now: 'Female Medic among the Dead, Unable to Man the Mortar'. I will always upset someone along the path that I have chosen, and that someone can continue to battle it out on their own call of duty battlefield. Weak if I die while surrounded by munitions; wrong if I use those munitions because I choose to survive.

After the death of my brother David, I knew that I would never allow myself to become a victim; and if there was ever an opportunity for me to do something – anything – to avoid that, I would take that opportunity. I would do whatever was necessary to avoid it. That is still true for me; it always will be.

As the number two on the mortar, my role is to prime (or arm) mortar rounds for Davey. I have been trained on how to use the weapon system, learning to do so during another course at the ITC in Brecon. It is a small weapon, easily man-packable, and often used if the Taliban attack at night. The team fire what we call 'para-illum', which, at a fixed height, detonates and lights up the night sky. Its powerful flare lasts for almost thirty seconds, allowing the Jocks to identify the location of enemy fighters hiding under the cover of darkness.

There was a time when it would have been unheard of for a medic to man the mortar line, times are a-changing. The Jocks aren't concerned: it doesn't matter what cap badge you wear so long as you can do the job. The days of definitive front lines are over; this is a 360-degree battlefield. My time in Marjah has already proved that every soldier must be prepared to engage the enemy, or at least be capable of reacting to any given situation. I am grateful for the hideous training that I have put myself through prior to this deployment. Spending much time with Paul Scott, a sergeant in 2 PARA's support company, I learnt all about support weapon systems from him, including how to employ them within a company group. His skill helped to shape mine, and with his guidance, I passed both basic tactics and our military senior range qualification courses. Tactics with distinction, the other 'scraping' an A grade. Scotty joked on my return that if I had been a paratrooper, I would have passed both with distinction. I was, and still am, grateful that he took the time to teach me.

He must have gotten something right, because here I am in Helmand Province, about to embark on my first mortar mission. It's a hesitant one. As Davey fires, I nervously hand him mortar rounds from the crate next to me, making sure that the safety pin is pulled off the side of the nose fuse (that's the way that the bombs are armed before firing).

We work well together. I practice firing when using the illuminated flares or smoke rounds, and this makes sure that I get it right when firing high explosive (HE) rounds. We smash through several crates before coming across a crate of duff mortars, ineffective perhaps from heat damage. Setting them aside, I call for another crate.

The time I spend on the 51 mm takes my mind off the depressing reality of how many casualties we are taking. The CAP is always my top priority, but this secondary task gives me something other than blood to focus on.

PB Argyll is under attack now, and Davey and I hurry out to our pit. Straight into it, Maj. Clark calls out, 'Five rounds from the 51! Fire for effect, Sergeant Major.' Off we go like a well-oiled machine. Within seconds, the boss sprints out of the CP, screaming for us to take cover. ICOM has identified that IDF is imminent.

Davey and I lay face down in the dirt, waiting for the incoming mortars or rockets to land. Out in the open ground, with no cover at all, sheltered only by my oversized helmet and the plates in my body armour, I think back to the moment when

I offered to help, wondering, *What the fuck was I thinking? Volunteering? Haven't I learnt anything?*

There by the grace of God go Davey and I. A great man, I have a lot of admiration for big Davey, mainly because he cares so much for his men. Their welfare is always his priority, and he makes sure that they know it. He is the bearer of all news, good and bad. Unscathed, we pack up our makeshift firing pit and head back to the CP.

A few hours later, Davey approaches me as I carry out some personal chores. He tells me that one of my section medics has been shot down in the Nawa district south of Lashkar Gah. We were there the week before this mayhem started. LCpl Andy James was one of my squadron's rising star's; he's been evacuated to Camp Bastion. The news puts our whole team on a downer. Of late, the days have brought us nothing but shit news. Andy was due to join us down here in Nad-e Ali. It could be worse though, at least he is alive.

I retire to my roll mat for some much-needed quiet time. A quick hour should do the trick. Closing my eyes, I fall into the deepest sleep. Ten minutes in, and the PB is hit again. 'For fuck's sake,' I mutter, waking like a bear, with a sore head, body armour intact, and helmet straight on. Rounds ping their way through the ops room windows, this time ricocheting around the room.

A young Jock narrowly missed yells out, 'Ah, well... better luck next time, ya fuckin' bawbags!'

Flashheart is up and about, clutching his red iPod.

'You okay, sir?' I ask before lying back on my roll mat.

'I'm always okay, Sgt T,' he says with a smile.

'Red iPod okay?' I say.

No reply this time, just an awkward smile followed by an awkward silence.

Capt. Wood laughs in the corner before mumbling, 'Man-crush.'

The jokes and abuse keep everyone grounded, and after a truly desperate couple of days, I wonder how much more we can take. We have two platoons of men who aren't fully manned, and we have no OMLT to mentor the worn-out kandak.

Four soldiers are dead so far, and we count ourselves lucky that we haven't lost more. The boss orders another no-patrol day tomorrow, and the news is most welcome. Flashheart and his now combat-ineffective team will await the arrival of the new OMLT, just as B Company will await the arrival of the first elements of 42 Commando. The kandak will remain in place until further notice; not a nice prospect to face, but they carry on regardless. I remember meeting the OC of Lima Company, 42 Commando, which would replace us in Lash. He was on the advance reconnaissance package that units do prior to deployment, which gives an indication about ground covered, future intentions, and all of the other good stuff that make up the 'big picture'. We Brits always do our recce way too early; a lot can change in a few days, let alone weeks.

By the time these guys turn up, their AO is completely different from what they were briefed back home. We deployed on a familiarisation patrol around Lash district centre, covering all noteworthy points. Towards the end of the patrol, we encountered a suicide bomber dressed in a burqa. The Afghan police shot him dead before he could detonate very close to Governor Gulab Mangal's compound. The burqa was bright pink, a very unusual choice of colour for these parts, paired with glitter-emblazoned high heels. In short, it was not the low-profile suicide bomber that I was expecting. Identified as a male, he couldn't walk properly in the heels that he wore, which first attracted attention and then quickly sparked suspicion.

Non-cooperation to verbal warning orders led to a burst from an AK-47 assault rifle.

Heading straight to Nad-e Ali, Lima Company of 42 Commando are in for an interesting start to their tour.

CHAPTER 8

ALI CAT

ADVANCE PERSONNEL FROM 3 COMMANDO BRIGADE ARE inbound this morning, and my first thought is how disappointed they will be when they realise that the shower is out of bounds. Having served in support of members of 42 Commando in Sierra Leone, I am well acquainted with their unique practices. (They provided force protection for our small team when deploying to the more rugged areas upcountry.)

Marines are definitely a different breed. My grandfather was a Royal Marine, and he fought in Korea. Buck Taylor was part of 'the Raiders' 41 Independent Commando, and his unit suffered great losses. When he chatted of his time in Korea, he spoke quietly of the day that involved a daylight raid into the area of Sonjin. Many of his close friends never made it home. Nothing can make up for that loss, but 41 Independent Commando were awarded an American Presidential unit citation in 1957. Extremely proud of his days as a Commando, Buck was buried in his much-loved Green Beret, and his regimental blazer was rarely off his back.

My grandfather passed away in 1999 at the age of seventy-four, not old in today's terms. Serving on operations in Kosovo at the time, I received a letter from him soon after he passed; he must have written it before he died. I read it time and time again, enjoying the way that he wrote. It was old fashioned, and our handwriting was exactly the same. He wrote in the letter that I should trust no one and never turn my back on the enemy. If I react I am to react with speed. He went on to quote from 'The Man in the Arena', an excerpt from a speech given by Theodore Roosevelt in 1910, shortly after his term as President of the United States [*see* this book's epigraph]. The junior medic in me had no real understanding of what any of my grandfather's letter meant – neither his own words nor the quoted speech. I laughed at the 'trust no one and react with speed' piece, just thinking he was an old-school war hero.

Afghanistan was where the penny finally dropped. Neither a grunt nor a man, a combat medic serving in support of a brigade, made up of the type of soldiers that he was talking about. The speech is about men like him, men who put themselves out there, men who push themselves and aren't afraid of the prospect of failure. With all the action in Nad-e Ali came plenty of quiet time, often tending thoughts of family and close friends and how much they meant to me. I feel extremely proud of my grandfather, but I never got the chance to tell him. They don't make them like him anymore; he didn't blame an ex-wife or poor upbringing for the few issues that he had. Nowadays people don't want to take any responsibility – it always has to be someone else's fault. He signed his letter '*Semper Fi*'. I would hear this again, many years later from my comrades of the US Marine Corps. I look at my own faults, and, like most people, I have plenty. For the most part, though, they make me who I am. It took me a while to take responsibility for being impatient, sometimes unwavering. It's fair to say I am fiery in nature, and before I can stop myself, words have usually already fallen from my lips. My dad taught me that a strong offence is the best defence. Maybe I take that too literally at times. However, if we were all the same, life would be a flat line. Not immune to diving straight off a fence, I don't always land on the safe side. That's just who I am.

When my grandfather spoke about trusting no one and not turning my back on the enemy, I smiled, thinking, *When will I ever be face-to-face with the enemy?* Maybe Marjah was what he was talking about. I hadn't planned to engage or kill anyone that day, but sometimes you are forced into the 'arena', whether you like it or not. It's the action you take that will often decide your fate; an element of luck can be useful at times too. I don't pretend to know all the answers, but my grandfather's wisdom makes me ask tough questions, and sometimes that's the best and the most we can do.

I wonder why betrayal happens to us. The coalition forces have been so trusting of our allies. Sometimes there's no choice but to be trusting. Both we Brits and the Americans have been hit hard by trusted Afghans who in some cases have worked alongside us for many years. I believe that this was the very type of enemy that my grandfather referred to. I think he meant that I should trust when I had to, but never fully – especially when dealing with a society that is very different from our own.

Thinking about my grandfather makes me think fondly of the Commandos. They have their own quirks, some of which are almost ritualistic, like their shower fetish. Wake up, shower, go for a run, shower, have a lunchtime nap, possible shower to refresh, afternoon gym session, shower, and bedtime. Showering is clearly the primary activity. That certainly won't be the case here. With water at a premium, the grunts and attached arms usually opt for the much-loved '3 PARA shower', which means clean nothing, or do the bare minimum.

Support elements from the incoming unit will be first to arrive, but it's unclear how the main body will arrive. According to the boss, a move by air is the most probable. We will hand over our vehicles and equipment just the same as we would have back in the PRT compound.

I notice today that the temperature has dropped. The majority of the soldiers in Argyll are taking a well-earned rest, enjoying the cooler weather. Abbie and I sit chatting outside the CAP having a cup of tea and enjoying some 'biscuits fruit'. The military sometimes describe things in a weird, backward fashion. Any normal person would surely say 'fruit biscuits'. They aren't dissimilar to the old-school Garibaldi biscuits, the ones that your dad normally likes, right up there with Jamaica cake or corned beef.

After twenty or so minutes, Abbie spots something moving about underneath the WMIK sitting directly in front of us. She climbs underneath to investigate, finding a tiny friendly call sign. 'It's a kitten!' she says. The little thing is foraging in a discarded ration box, probably looking for food. Abbie manages to lift the animal out from its shelter, delighted by the tiny ball of fur.

Brought up around dogs, I never really had time for cats. Kosovo was the first time that I had any type of association with one. We adopted a tiny black-and-white kitten, and he would often sleep on my camp cot while I was out. His company became routine, and I liked having him around. In our world of ever-increasing absurdity, we named him Scooby after the huge cartoon dog Scooby Doo. The very British satire of Monty Python is evident in most soldiers; it's the irony of the shitty situations in which you find yourself that often get you through. Our cat was euthanised by an overzealous environmental health technician. I didn't show it at the time, but I was angry that the little man had been killed. He was a welcome distraction for the medics coming back from the horror of assisting the Canadians with the exhumation of mass graves. Sometimes soldiers at the forefront see a very different picture than those who serve in the rear echelons.

Animals provide a source of normality in what are very abnormal circumstances. So long as you don't start cutting about like Dr Doolittle, I see no harm in keeping animals around camp. Common sense says that you can't have wild packs of dogs running around a base or snakes climbing over camp cots like something out of the *Jungle Book*.

I presume the cat Abbie found is a male. She gives him some water, and after all this time, I finally find a worthwhile purpose for my army ration pâté. The kitten loves it, and I am delighted to have found a legitimate reason not to eat it. It sounds more professional to say that I need to feed the cat than to offer my usual 'it tastes like shit' excuse. We name him Ali Cat because he is a survivor of Nad-e Ali.

Ali Cat becomes a permanent fixture in and around the ops room, much to the disapproval of the boss, who even forced Davey to show his compassionate side. We would often find the sergeant major playing with or feeding him. Just the previous week, Davey unintentionally traumatised himself with an incident involving another cat in the PB. Ham found a kitten that was far smaller than Ali Cat, even smaller than my hand; in fact, you could only just make out its tiny features. Initially the main effort was to find its mum. We searched every inch of the base – gun positions, toilet block, and so on – but there was no sight of her. I found it strange that a nursing mum would go so far away from a newborn, but maybe this was the way that cats rolled in Afghanistan. With the situation unfolding, everyone on camp decided to become the resident expert in wild cat behaviour. 'I can offer advice on how to be "feral" if that is any use, people.' After much discussion, the overall consensus was that Mum isn't coming back.

We tried to nurse the kitten ourselves, using small syringes to feed it. The culturally different Afghans looked at us, wondering why we were bothering – it was just a cat, after all. I realised then that with so much destruction around them, the blokes needed an outlet to show kindness to. This is still true, and now we have a new kitten. Ali Cat might help mend the mental scarring that in some will be inevitable, and these small slices of humanity are what make us different from our Afghan counterparts.

The Jocks won't hesitate when pushing a bayonet into another human being, but they will always show compassion and kindness to casualties of war, including animals. It's the children of war whom soldiers normally reach out to; their innocence will sometimes uplift the desperate and unforgiving reality of battle. There are no youngsters in Nad-e Ali. In fact, we are using their school as a PB.

The Jocks never show that they are bothered by our circumstances, but during quiet times showing some affection to a small kitten isn't so uncool, and it gives them something to think about other than killing the Taliban. Recalling our efforts with the first kitten, I hope Ali Cat will fare better. All attempts to feed the newborn proved fruitless, and it would have been cruel to leave it to die in the heat. Making milk from the powder in the sachets from our ration packs, we tried everything. It was not a shock when the kitten rejected every attempt. Deciding on its fate, we agreed that we should put the newborn out of its misery, leaving the sergeant major with the unenviable task. I don't want to think about it, so I just convince myself that Ali Cat is bigger and stronger, and all will be well.

Life goes on at PB Argyll. As the Jocks continue to probe Shin Kalay, our daily jaunts are becoming increasingly perilous. Firmly into battle routine, the base soaks up the daily attacks. Together with Davey, I continue to support the lads with use of the 51. Scotty Pew's gun team on the roof provide our lifeline: he directs us on the mortar, monitoring our fall of shot. Any doubts that I had about helping out have all but faded. With every one of us in the PB embracing our tasks, my medics support every operation that happens, whether inside or outside of Argyll.

Just when it seems that our luck is turning, B Company faces a further blow. The boss announces that Monty is required back at our MOB in Lash: he will brief the incoming Commandos on what's happening down here. It's a necessary evil, but that doesn't soften the blow for us losing him. Monty will be replaced at some point by Sgt Damian ('Damo') Partridge. Damo has already been bloodied this tour, and it will be good to see his chirpy face. Until his arrival, though, 2Lt Du Boulay will lead the platoon alone.

B Company men are battle worn; it's been a long summer, and the young section commanders are all ageing well beyond their years. The experience that all of us have accumulated is far more than any course will ever teach us. I wonder where we will go from here. Soldiering doesn't get any better than it is now; other operations will surely pale into insignificance.

The new faces arriving will hold the line through the winter. There are no new medics as yet, but we're informed that they will arrive along with the main body. A doctor will head the team up.

'Better late than never,' I grumble to Kev.

With the incoming marines, banter has already started. The language barrier between them and the Jocks is making for an interesting handover. The inbound grunts will be enjoying their scran, as opposed to scoff, and a cup of tea is known as a wet and not a brew.

The Jocks' nurturing almost permissive nature suggests that they are always open to new ideas. As Ferris explains it, 'I dunni give a fuck who's takin' over, just get the cunts here.' His take on the handover is resonated throughout the company, such a beautiful way with words, almost poetic. The spirit of a young Jock is infectious: they have nothing to prove and everything to gain, and at their worst, they are probably at their best. 'If you are hangin' oot yer arse, then at least have the decency to do it with panache, eh!' Words of wisdom from Ham, still cutting about on his ATV.

A message comes through from my higher echelon at Camp Bastion. Jen and I will fly back to Lash a couple of days before Abbie and Sean. Flights home are already booked, so names are non-negotiable. Our exit should be at least a few days away yet, so packing up won't start any time soon. We don't have too much kit here, just enough to make our backpacks uncomfortably heavy for the helicopter ride back to our MOB. Company 2IC Capt. Wood is on the same flight as we are; he, too, is required to work with the marines during the handover phase. The boss isn't over enthused that we are all leaving. He tries to persuade HQ to leave us until the last helo out. Everyone's proven themselves, and with that comes trust, which takes a fair amount of time to build.

Another attack comes at sundown. All arcs are covered, and our retaliatory fire smashes the Taliban. With every assault on our base Scotty Pew's speed and precision of target acquisition is getting all the more impressive; somehow, though, the enemy's numbers remain. As the dusk attack comes to an end, so does my own mission on the 51, and I make my way back into the CP. I have gotten so used to the sounds of munitions that I am often tempted just to sack off taking cover. Complacency is harder to fight than the enemy at times. Prolonged exposure to combat causes fatigue, and with that, poor judgement may follow. It's the time that personal discipline must kick in, with rounds freely pinging around our base at all times of day. I don't want to be the Afghan who chose not to don his body armour.

Stripping down, I take off my soaking wet body armour. A dejected-looking OC stands in the doorway. 'Sgt T, can I have a word?' he says.

'No worries, sir, I will just be a second.'

Nervous, I have seen this look before, and I know bad news is about to follow. Automatically bracing myself for news of a family member, I dread what he is about to say.

'It's Ham,' Maj. Clark says.

I feel a mixture of confusion and relief as I follow the boss outside, realising my family is okay. Maj. Clark guides me around the side of the ops room so that we're out of earshot of the young Jocks.

'Ham's received some bad news from home,' the boss explains. 'His wife is very ill.'

He further explains that Ham is needed at home, and things are moving fast. With any type of immediate family sickness, the military are very effective and will pull out all the stops to get the affected soldier home. I find Ham sitting near the back wall outside the aid post. We are great friends, and I put my arms on his shoulders, pressing down tightly. Ham is like a brother to me, and I feel choked for him. It's the worst feeling in the world when you can't help a loved one, and it's hard to watch a friend suffer through it. This is especially true with Ham, who is usually a constant source of amusement.

Ham has a long journey ahead, and his situation brings to mind my own long trip home from Cyprus, where I had been on exercise when I received a phone call about my brother's condition. When I got back to the UK, it was just in time to turn David's life support machine off.

Ham will be flying from Nad-e Ali to Camp Bastion, Bastion to Kandahar, and then on to Kabul. His flight from Kabul is the longest stretch, and the one that he will suffer on. If there was a doctor here in Nad-e Ali, they would have taken care of it. I place one tablet in a small clear pill dispensing bag and give it to Ham, explaining that it will help him sleep on the longest leg of his journey. I write a small prescriptive note so Ham can use the pill if required. It's not normal practice, but these aren't normal circumstances.

For the hundredth time, I head back into the medical room. I look around at our mediocre set-up, unsure about how we have gotten through the last seven weeks.

Suddenly the OC reappears in the doorway. 'Sgt T, timings have been brought forward on account of Ham's situation, so you, LCpl Young, and the 2IC will be leaving Nad-e Ali in a few hours.'

At that very moment, my pulse quickens, bringing back my sweaty palms. I am completely freaked out at the thought of leaving. We have a sequence here; good or bad, it has worked. I feel awkward at the thought of going back to Lash, and I don't understand why we have to leave *now*.

'We should pack, Jen,' I say, breaking the silence.

Jen nods. She travels light, and out of all our team, her personal administration is by far the best. Everything has its place, and she doesn't care much for niceties.

It's not going to be easy leaving Abbie and Sean here, but we can't stay in Nad-e Ali forever. After a half hour or so, our packing is complete. Packs are moved outside the aid post onto the small pathway leading to the front gate. With the little time that we have, we make our way around the base to say goodbye to the Jocks on the wall.

I catch a glimpse of young Ptes Ferris and Cameron two junior Jocks whom I have known since their days as young recruits. Cam was a recruit in my platoon, and Ferris was part of another training company. His name was known across the training regiment for all the wrong reasons of course. I hand out any spare kit, and the gun position at the front gate gets my beloved speakers so they can enjoy music during the quiet times of the day. As the four of us prepare to make our way out to the HLZ for the last time, the threat on our birds comes to the forefront of my mind.

Maj. Clark is outside already. 'Sgt T, thanks for everything you have done. See you back at Lash soon.'

I get a hug from Davey. He laughs, acknowledging that, with me gone, he will man the 51 alone.

B Company commander shakes all of our hands before we set off. I always find this part a bit embarrassing; we Brits don't deal with accepting or giving praise very well. Doing your job well is the very least you can do.

Twilight shifts to night-time. Grabbing my weapon, I notice Ali Cat lying beside it. Picking up the little man for the last time is harder than I imagined.

'Anti-cat Taylor is going soft,' Abbie announces.

Looking back now, I realise that getting attached is something that I struggle with. I put much of my inability to want to get emotionally involved down to not dealing with David's death properly. No one thinks that what they dread most will ever happen to them – and we all go along thinking that the things that wind up hurting us the most will never happen, but, more often than not, they do. I recollect feeling guilty for wishing that it was someone else's brother who had died. It's so much easier to console others than it is to console yourself. It took a long time to recognise my grief. The books say recognition is the toughest part, so with a little help from Ali Cat, progress has been made.

Davey leads us out to the HLZ. The straps from my backpack dig deep into my now-scrawny frame (the Helmand diet is the best-kept secret in the world). Wheels are up from Camp Bastion. Kneeling in complete darkness, we listen for the sound of the Chinook, pondering if the Taliban will hit this time. The bird is inbound, and the four of us shelter each other as it swoops in. As always, the heat from the downdraught makes it hard to breathe. One by one, like pensioners, we clamber up with our heavy kit, making our way onto the back of the Chinook.

On last, I am left with nowhere to sit. I kneel with my heavy pack still on my back; rationale says that it's only going to be a short trip. I grab Jen's arm as we take off; not sure why, it just felt like the right thing to do. We are all aware that it's only a matter of time before one of our birds is shot out of the sky. Half an hour later the ramp is lowered on the back: we are at Camp Bastion to drop Ham off. As he goes by, I stick my hand out. He taps it, mouthing, 'Catch you later, mucker.'

The helicopter lifts again. Grabbing hold of a metal box, I steady myself. My right leg is numb, as I didn't take into consideration the drop-offs when I positioned myself. Almost there now, and the contents of my stomach leap up and down as the helicopter drops low and fast.

The pilots' aim is to evade potential rocket attacks. Skimming roofs of compounds on the approach to the MOB at Lashkar Gah is like a roller-coaster ride at night. The door gunner standing to the rear of the airframe lifts his NVG and taps my shoulder. As I look up, he points to his watch and gestures with two fingers, indicating that we will be on the ground in two minutes. I pass the info to Jen, who in turn passes it on to the next man.

Finally, wheels are down on the ground. The aircraft sits behind a high perimeter wall, giving it some degree of protection. The pilots are anxious to lift again, as staying put for any length of time increases the chance of attack tenfold. All pax are ushered off, and my dead leg is slow to react as I manoeuvre myself. The change in engine pitch signifies the lift. Taking cover, I instruct the civilian who joined the flight from Camp Bastion to face away from the bird. A face full of shingle-style pebbles would not have ended the day well. As the shadow of the Chinook disappears into the night sky, I see that our medical team are waiting for us: Doc Richards and Cpl Stevie Housden have waited up, and it's a relief to see their smiling faces.

My brain is still in PB mode, and I feel overwhelmed by the light and noise in the compound. At night, Argyll was usually in silence unless we were under attack. The sound of generators and the glare from the perimeter lights unsettle me.

Jen and I drop our kit off in the nine-foot-by-nine-foot canvas shelter that we left seven weeks prior. I head to the Internet cabin. It's late, so the terminals must be free. Jen heads to the shower block. To my delight, the Internet is down. I make my way back to our tent. Climbing through the small flap of canvas at the front, I hear a loud Scottish voice. 'Hey, hey, mucker.'

Turning, I see a figure moving very quickly towards me from out of the shadow. I realise it's my man Duffy. He lifts me off the ground, and his smiling face lights up. Young soldiers like Duffy are the ones who make these days away from home worthwhile. He doesn't fight for political gain or to hunt terror cells, he fights for his friends in the hope that they all make it home. Our so-called PlayStation generation has fought hard in Helmand and continues to do so. And for this moment alone, I am glad to have left Nad-e Ali.

CHAPTER 9

HOMEWARD BOUND

BACK IN LASHKAR GAH, TIRED AND DISHEVELLED, I LOOK down at my camp cot for the first time in seven weeks. Not as comfortable as my bed at home, it is still a world away from the thin roll mat I have left behind on the floor of the PB. I am exhausted, so drained that I completely sack off any notion of a shower – the last thing I want to feel is refreshed or awake. Trudging over to the toilet block with my toothbrush in hand, I make short work of an essential strip wash, managing to get back to my bed space within ten minutes. I don't care about anything other than sleeping.

My body's natural adrenaline from the daily attacks and copious amounts of casualties kept me going in Nad-e Ali, but now I feel like a zombie, the walking dead. Before Jen has a chance to put the light out, I am flat out and comatose. It's the deepest sleep that I can remember; not even stirring, I manage to stay out for a straight twelve hours. If I could bottle this exhaustion and sell it as a sleep aid, I would make millions.

Waking up is quite a different story: a major hangover headache, minus the alcohol. I am completely dehydrated, hungry, and dying for the toilet. With not a multipurpose yellow sharps container in sight, I trek out to the lavatory. I get eyes on myself in the mirror, and what I see is hideous. Looking at the huge dark circles around my usually smiling Irish eyes, I am horrified. My skin is like leather to the touch, and I look completely weather-beaten. I figure that I have lost about twenty-five pounds in weight, and I now resemble the Tom Hanks character in the film *Castaway*, minus the beard. My combats are hanging off my arse, and I won't deny that this is a welcome sight.

Relaxing at last, I enjoy the tranquillity of the shower block; using a toilet without the worry of a murder hole is all of a sudden a significant event in my life, and for the first time in weeks I feel safe. Nad-e Ali is raw and untamed: it's a world away from the MOB here in Lash. It takes an absolute age to scrub myself clean, as the grime is embedded all over me. I stay in the shower for over an hour, trying to zone out and get back to reality.

I keep thinking about Abbie and Sean. Ali Cat must wonder where I have gone. He slept on top of my bivvy bag at night, and I liked the sensation of his little paws climbing over me to get comfy. He would try to move stealthily, stalking shadows in the room before tumbling over. It's hard to believe all that is behind me now.

I head back to the tent. Jen and I each finally get into a clean set of combats. She starts packing as I endeavour to find out information about our flights home. It won't be long now. The PRT begins to fill up with personnel from 3 Commando Brigade.

Going along the walkways, I barely recognise people as I pass them. Just outside the regimental aid post (RAP), I spot Capt. Wood. He looks as dishevelled as I do. 'Sleep well, Sgt T?' he asks. 'When will you head to Bastion?'

'Too well, sir,' I say in response to his first question, adding in response to the second, 'Just waiting for timings, but we're out of here tomorrow morning. We'll move on to Cyprus a couple of days after that.'

'Come up to the ops room before you leave,' he says. 'Monty is briefing the marines, and Flashheart is cutting about.'

'Thanks, I will,' I reply. Double knee pads pop into my head as I continue to walk along the stone path to the clinic. Chuckling to myself at the thought of Flashheart and his antics around the base, I make my way into the medical reception. Maj. Richards, our doc, lets me know that we are moving to Camp Bastion after first light tomorrow morning.

With no time to spare, I must start packing. I look forward to starting my trip home, but I have to make the rounds before I go. Firstly, B Company ops room: it's good to see some of the guys again. News that Ham made it back home in fewer than twenty-four hours is most welcome.

Being away from the PB has left a void in my routine, and I am in danger of becoming one of those 'mincers', people who dwell upon where they have been and what they have done. I like life, and I'm in desperate need to get back to it. Nad-e Ali was over for me, and now I just want to get home so I can see my fiancé and family.

A trip to the quartermaster's department brings me crashing straight back into regimental reality. Handing back kit that I have signed for turns into an epic fail, as watching staff finish off games of solitaire before signing me off raises the issue of my patience – or lack of it. Back to the ops room I go, where I see Flashheart and his red iPod. Solitaire guy is forgotten, and the visual of Flash sends me into a laughing fit. Marines in the ops room look at him in disbelief; they don't get the joke about the red iPod, either. Regardless, coffee press in hand, we head to the cookhouse for food.

My new sense of purpose makes the day race by. Our first stop will be Camp Bastion, where I can catch up with friends who have been deployed to different bases upcountry. I can also get an update on Abbie and Sean from the main medical ops room. Before saying goodbye, emails are exchanged, all of us hoping that we will see one another again someday.

Finally, I head back to my tent to pack and have one last sleep. Once I'm all packed, my head hits the pillow. I'm out early, ready for another undisturbed night.

Just before first light, Jen and I make our way to the HLZ. It's busy with people waiting to fly to Camp Bastion, as the bird drops in, kit and equipment are placed on in the centre of the airframe. Personnel file up each side and then buckle in to the seats. The Chinook is airborne, so the first leg of our trip home has started.

Camp Bastion is as busy as ever, with helicopters coming in from every location. We drive past the airhead which houses all of the Ugly call signs (or Apaches). There's never an opportunity to thank the pilots of these incredible machines; to us on the ground, they are just another faceless call sign, albeit a very important one.

When we arrive at our medical HQ, we are met by squadron Sgt Maj. Justin Harris. 'Glad to see you lot are okay. The PB was hit hard last night. Three of the lads have been shot on PB Argyll.'

Taken aback, my cheerfulness is short-lived. I need confirmation, so I manage a choked, 'No KIA?'

'No fatalities,' Sgt Maj. Harris confirms. 'The lads are over in the hospital. They were all shot inside the perimeter wall. A company of marines are deploying a couple of days early; the Taliban are all over that area.'

Dropping off our kit, Jen and I head straight for the hospital to check in on our guys. The three of them were wearing body armour, so with no head shots, they escaped the attack with only wounded limbs.

Just to jump ahead briefly, here is how events in Nad-e Ali played out. When 42 Commando eventually replaced B Company of 5 Scots, airdrops of rations and water were being made, much landing too far into enemy-held areas to safely retrieve. The district would need a force of more than 1,500 soldiers to stabilise it. Operation Sond Chara ('Red Dagger' in Pashto) was an eighteen-day campaign with objectives centred on four Taliban strongholds near the town of Nad-e Ali. The op was named after the commando insignia worn by members of 3 Commando Brigade; 1,500 British troops were involved, supported by Danish, Estonian, and Afghan forces in the pre-Christmas offensive.

The offensive was to make safe the area around the Helmand capital of Lashkar Gah. After an ever-increasing amount of insurgent attacks, the Taliban had planned to overrun the provincial capital with a three-hundred-strong force. The initial defence of Nad-e Ali cost five British soldiers, including an Australian on secondment to the Brits; the Afghan body count is unknown.

The bloody battles fought by the commandos put into perspective what B Company had achieved: holding Nad-e Ali against all odds, and somehow managing to subdue a very determined enemy. I felt proud, then and now, to have been a part of it. Nad-e Ali contained both the worst and best times of my military career.

Back to the present, Camp Bastion is a hive of activity: the relief in place (RIP) is in full motion. The commando brigade anxiously waits to get stuck into their tour, while our battle-worn brigade simultaneously starts the draw-down. We will grieve for our fallen when we get home.

Walking through the tented camp on my way to the coffee shop, I see my old friend Phil Train (2 PARA). He has been based in the notorious district of Sangin, and it's a relief to see that he is okay. Like me, he has lost a fair amount of weight. We chat about our experiences housed in different locations, and he laughs when I tell him about my escapades in Nad-e Ali.

Time presses on, so I leave Phil and head over to our internal squadron quartermaster department to hand in my ammunition. Dreading another epic failure to move as quickly as I would like, I empty my magazines and have each clip of ammo ready for inspection. That way, the storeman can't mess up the count; ten rounds per clip, how hard can it be? It takes longer to get out of country than it does to get in. Flights are always delayed and kit is usually missing on the way out; never on the way in, though.

Our next move is to board the Hercules transport plane to Kandahar Air Force Base (KAF). The US Marines and elements of the 10th Mountain Division came here in late November 2001, when coalition forces first entered Afghanistan.

The base has expanded into a small city, housing more than 30,000 multinational troops. The population consumes nearly 37,000 gallons (140,000 litres) of water and 50,000 meals a day at six different military restaurants. Seen as far away from the front line of Helmand, Kandahar is the home of the Taliban and suffers from regular rocket attacks resulting in numerous KIA and casualties. Step outside the wire, and it's game on.

Prince William, our future head of the armed forces, has made several trips to Kandahar. I recall teaching him all about haemorrhage control during his pre-deployment training package back in the UK. Teaching several groups, I didn't recognise him until he approached me as the lesson came to an end.

'Thanks, Sgt Taylor, that was very informative,' he said.

Taking hold of his outstretched hand, I replied, 'Thanks, sir, have a safe trip.' I was rather embarrassed for not recognising him.

A very senior royal, it would be inappropriate for him to take part in offensive operations; however, his presence in theatre is always most welcome. British troops have the utmost respect for him and his younger brother, Prince Harry. Travelling to Kandahar always reminds me of Prince William.

Jen and I will spend the night here at the airbase. The site amazes me. Our American comrades certainly know how to go to war; they often bear the brunt of bad publicity about their overzealous use of force, but the truth is, they give more to these causes than anyone else in the world. We would not have functioned in Helmand if it weren't for the use of American assets. Our politicians are writing cheques that we as a small, well-trained military cannot possibly cash. US helicopters are possibly our biggest saviours in our fight to secure Helmand, not forgetting the uplift in troops that the marine expeditionary units provided for us.

Our morning departure is here in a flash, and after a quick shower, I indulge in an all-American breakfast. The dining facility (DEFAC) is the US version of our cookhouse; its purpose is to feed soldiers, but that's where the similarity ends. This place is unbelievable: seven hot plates serving a variety of food to cater to the many different nations based here. There are fridges full of every type of drink that you can think of, the latest coffee machines, and a quick-order bar if you fancy something fresh. They have absolutely everything! After gorging myself on pancakes and syrup, I roll out of the DEFAC. Bouncing from the sugar rush, off we go to the departures area of the airfield.

As my kit is loaded onto the back of one of many four-ton trucks, I am promptly reminded of an incident that very nearly sent me home early on. During the initial weeks of this tour, B Company was tasked with a forty-eight-hour deliberate op to the area of Babaji, north of Lashkar Gah. It's a district renowned for poppy cultivation, and the American-funded poppy eradication force (PEF) had been operating in the area for some time. Sustaining multiple casualties, they were in imminent danger of being overrun. The PEF were all over the place, getting hit at every opportunity. We were sent to provide a screen for them to move safely out of the area. I was excited at the thought of getting amongst it so soon into the tour.

We were moving by helicopter to Camp Bastion, where we would be met by the Viking crews, manned by Royal Marines. Using their tracked vehicles, we would manoeuvre to Babaji. After flying in from Lash, we transferred straight onto the back of four-ton trucks, just like the one that is now taking my kit home. As we rode along, I sat chatting to the grunt next to me. Suddenly and without warning, the side of the vehicle came away and the lad next to me and I both were thrown to the ground, hard bodies crashing onto the road. Landing on my back and winded from the fall, I could barely breathe. Thinking that I had some serious injury and unable to move, I lay still for what seemed like an eternity.

I kept thinking about the months spent doing hideous infantry training courses, getting beasted on all the shit training areas that the British military had to offer, and only managing to escape Otterburn. That entire effort coming to end so early on in my deployment because I fell out of the side of a moving four-ton truck was unthinkable. 'No fucking way!' I said, lying there like a grounded turtle and looking up at Jen and Sean standing over me.

An ambulance arrived at the scene, and I managed to get to my feet, not realising that I was going into shock. Medics always make the worst patients, as I've said. I was still struggling to breathe, and my body felt like I had been hit by a train. Miraculously, I had sustained no serious injuries. This was the story of my life: I was always hurting myself enough to make tasks extremely uncomfortable but never enough to stop me from doing them. I spent the entire mission in agony, the right side of my body purple and black from bruising. To add to my woes, this was my first encounter with my company commander.

It was not the initial impression that I had hoped to give our OC, Maj. Harry Clark, so early on in the tour. One positive did come from my early setback, though: Babaji became the birthplace of my multipurpose yellow sharps container.

I chuckle to myself at the memory, focusing again on the present moment. Our lives are now in the hands of the RAF. A movement sergeant stands on a box in the middle of the tent, shouting, 'Sirs, ma'ams, ladies, and gents... there has been a change of plan, and your flight is delayed!' the well-versed sergeant reveals. It's the same old shit that you hear every time you deploy anywhere. 'Tea and coffee are available in the dining facility. No weapons allowed, I'm afraid,' he adds.

A soldier standing next to me says that bags need to be checked in at 1600 hours. This is interesting, considering that our flight is at 0200 hours tomorrow morning.

With time on our hands, we opt to take a wander around KAF, heading straight for the post exchange (PX) so that we can indulge in some retail therapy. The PX is like a mini supermarket for the US military, selling everything from watches to televisions, to clothing, to perfume. Staring at all of the niceties, I opt for a Suunto Core Ops watch, excited that it has a built-in compass.

When I first came to KAF in 2006, the base was already well established; here again in 2008, the place is unbelievable, a hive of military activity. It has an area of half a square mile, complete with covered walkways and some interesting stores. For example, a German military shop sells souvenir burqas. I'm not sure why I would feel the need to take one home – perhaps it would be useful as part of an escape-and-evasion plan. At five feet, eight inches, I am too tall to be an Afghan woman, so I am better suited to the male kameez, with a loosely wrapped lungee, or Afghan turban, on my head, than a burqa. An untrained eye could be fooled for thirty seconds or more by me in a kameez/lungee costume. I laugh at the thought as we continue exploring the PX.

With coffee shops, a Burger King, and a Thai restaurant, the PX appears to add an air of normality against the backdrop of Black Hawks, C-130s, and Apaches. It's hard to explain how, but it just didn't seem right: with all this luxury, we were in danger of relaxing too much. The mindset of soldiers cutting about on mountain bikes appeared weird, and it was very different from the mindset of those in Helmand. We walk around like tourists, drinking our frappes in silence. I know that we are all going through the same process; everyone returning from Helmand probably feels the same way. Maybe that's what all the delays are designed for – they allow us to take gradual steps before hitting the streets of the UK.

As the sun begins to disappear, it is again time to indulge in the culinary delights of the DEFAC, where I stuff my face. Soon after, we are ushered onto coaches heading to the terminal. The journey is interrupted by loud sirens indicating that the base is under attack. IDF is very accurate in KAF, and I won't be taking any chances so close to getting home. Helmet and body armour go on, and straight into cover I go. Once the all-clear is given, we continue on with our journey to the terminal.

Lining up to check in, I amuse myself by studying the cabinet of weapons and illegal items that people have tried to take home. A grenade, bits of rifles, 7.62 mm rounds, swords, and pistols. The words 'full retard' pop into my head as I think about the type of clown that would try to take this stuff through the security checks. I can imagine the scene as the idiot tries to explain to the RAF police searching our kit:

'Well, I decided that this RPG would look good in my room back in the sergeants' mess!'

'Really? Is that what you thought?'

Next we get our passports and British army IDs checked by RAF flight staff, and we enjoy a further two-hour delay due to a snag in the missile decoy system. Past caring, I am just happy to be sitting on a plane that is homeward bound. Putting my body armour and helmet on with a grumble, I ponder what possible benefit I am going to get by placing this cumbersome outdated kit on. If our plane goes down or crashes with a full tank of fuel, there is a strong possibility that my Mark 6 Alpha helmet is probably not going to make it.

Within seconds, I am asleep, and then, a few hours later, we are landing in Cyprus. A convoy of coaches moves us to the camp that will house us for the evening. Morning breaks and tunnel beach awaits us. We swim, drink beer, and eat decent food. Lying in the sun and looking out to the deep blue sea, all my troubles begin to fade away. Like all fun tasks provided by the military, though, we have to partake in the standard swim test first. A few minutes of treading water before a hundred-metre swim will guarantee that I don't drown while enjoying the watersport section of organised fun. The British military is very good at draining the fun aspect from most sporting activities.

The two beers I have go straight to my head, leaving me feeling tired and tipsy. This type of decompression is a good time to catch up with friends. Chatting away until the early hours, I fall asleep and look forward to boarding the plane for the final leg home. Morning comes, and it's another coach ride. I get comfortable, ensuring that my iPod is fully charged. Boarding the flight, I secure a window seat for the longest leg of the journey. I am relieved that I won't wake up dribbling all over a complete stranger.

Landing at Stansted Airport is painless. Close to Colchester, England's oldest recorded town, it makes for an easy bus ride home. For once, baggage collection goes smoothly; this might have something – or everything – to do with the fact that the RAF isn't controlling it. Passengers for 16 Air Assault Brigade are ushered onto waiting coaches. For the first time in over six months, I ponder nothing. I have six months left of military service, and I am excited about the future.

As a medical commander, I am more relaxed than ever. I have learnt a great deal and am eager to pass it on before I close the book on my military life. I know that the months ahead will be busy. On all levels, 16 Close Support Medical Regiment is far more advanced when it comes to training its medics. The unit was formed in 1999 from the amalgamation of 19 Airmobile Field Ambulance and 23 Parachute Field Ambulance. Between the two units, they had been involved in every major operation since World War II.

After the union, the regiment saw action in Sierra Leone, Bosnia, Kosovo, Iraq, and, most recently, Afghanistan. The unit provides dedicated medical support to 16 Air Assault Brigade and will be called upon to support the complete spectrum of air assault operations. This includes airmobile, helicopter, and parachute deployments. A percentage of the regiment must be parachute trained to support the on-call readiness force, known as the Airborne Task Force (ABTF).

Two regular air assault medical surgical groups each provide role 2 medical support and resuscitative surgery. In addition to the regular squadrons, the regiment is bolstered by a territorial army (TA) squadron. The 144 Parachute Medical Squadron is a permanent part of the brigade, and it is based in London, Cardiff, Glasgow, and Nottingham. The TA squadron is fully integrated, and members deploy regularly on operations and exercises in support of the brigade.

The majority of the professionals and skills of the army medical services can be found within the organisation, and 16 Brigade is fortunate enough to be staffed with the best physicians that the military has to offer, most going on to support UK Special Forces. Combat medics posted in the brigade are highly motivated. The will to succeed and be the very best is echoed throughout the ranks, and my success now has much to do with my time serving in this unit. The thought of someday leaving the brigade solidified my decision to leave the service. Unlike the infantry, medics are posted every three years, and I didn't embrace the option of being sent anywhere else.

Arriving home on leave, I initially spend quality time with my fiancé, Ryan. We book a last-minute holiday, ending up somewhere in the Greek Islands. Shocked at the distance from top to bottom, our villa is halfway up the side of a mountain.

'The brochure said foothills of Nisaki!' Ryan laughs.

'Look at the car,' I add. 'A burnt-orange Fiat Uno.'

It's the wrong time of year for this place: our swimming pool is ice-cold, and we have a view of Albania halfway up the side of something resembling Everest Basecamp. Not the relaxing bolthole I envisioned. I nickname our villa 'PB Nisaki'. After renaming our crap car a Fiat Oh-No, we set about having a good time.

Our personal relationship is failing: the best of friends, two tours of Helmand later, and our private lives have turned into a military exercise. I desperately want to move on and give some years to a life outside. Ryan had joined 3 PARA at seventeen years old, so I couldn't expect him to give that up.

Catching up with family is very important to me. I haven't told a soul about my time in Nad-e Ali; I've buried it like most other soldiers do.

Stupidly, I concentrate on drinking and getting back into what I think is some kind of normality. The operations that I was a part of have changed my outlook on life: I learnt to consider it normal to think that every day might be my last. Thinking this way is necessary for survival in a war zone, but in day-to-day life, it's far from normal, and usually a classic symptom of PTSD.

Thinking about what the future might hold starts to fill me with apprehension. Facing so many changes at once, my mind starts working overtime. The things that I experienced in Afghanistan began to hit me all at once.

As I prepare to leave the military, I feel unsure that I am making the right decision, doubtful that I will be able to cope with the lack of routine. I am taking a gamble by leaving the army that saved me when I was a twenty-two-year-old lacking direction.

Selected for promotion and recommended to commission as an officer from the ranks, I come top of my promotion board in an airborne unit. For any medic, this is a huge achievement, and aside from my regimental sergeant major, I have attained status as the most-qualified medic tactically within my regiment. In a strange way, this makes me feel safe; I'm in a world where I will be looked after.

I spend my final months in the unit training personnel for upcoming operations. Sent to Germany along with a small group, I deliver intensive battlefield training to a medical unit there, but they weren't overly keen taking instruction. Units are competitive, and taking advice based on our experience seems to be unwelcome in some quarters. Just as I frowned upon infantry courses run in Germany and not ITC Brecon, they frown upon the likes of me taking charge of their range practices. As I noted earlier, basic soldiering is key, and if you don't know the fundamentals at this stage of the game, I sure as shit don't have the time to teach back week one, day one.

CHAPTER 10

SAYING GOODBYE

AN INFORMAL GATHERING OF UNIT PERSONNEL IN THE squadron hangar is the scene for all goodbyes, presentations, and speeches. Without much thought, I roll in, almost forgetting that this time it's my farewell. Not overly keen on any fuss being made, I smile through the speeches given by friends and my sergeant major. (Even now, looking back, I can't recall any of the words spoken.) I receive a brown box, a framed picture, and a black issued day sack (small backpack) covered in flowers. I am an avid black day sack hater, and have been ever since the day I first spotted one sitting awkwardly on the back of one of our junior soldiers.

The black day sack is a hideous, non-value-adding piece of kit, as is the individual carrying it. There's a pocket made from some form of netted material on the front of the bag, so recruits in training can place a piece of white paper inside with their name on it. Basic training is the only time that the inoperable piece of kit should ever be seen. Experienced soldiers have no business carrying it.

During the countless exercises that I have put my medical squadron through. We have become soldiers who carry med packs, not medics who carry weapons. I feel proud of the tactical discipline instilled in the squadron, but, more importantly, happy that all of our forward-operating medics came home safe to their families after our last tour of Helmand Province. Looking around at the smiling faces of the young medics in front of me, I reckon that the black day sack may have just become my legacy.

The framed picture is a smaller version of a huge print that sits proudly in the training wing of 16 Air Assault Brigade: it's a photo of me and another soldier assisting an Afghan casualty in Lashkar Gah in 2008. Not bothering to open the box, I am sure it's the usual gift of a carved figure of a field medic. Heading back to the sergeants' mess, I continue to pack up the remainder of my things. Shipping my life back to Devon is proving to be a sizeable undertaking. Laughing at the flowery black day sack I place it, along with the framed picture, into one of my huge cardboard boxes.

Sitting on the side of my bed, I open the small brown box to see if the statue has changed in any way since my last one. Unfolding the bubble wrap, I can feel that the gift is not the figure of a soldier at all. Pulling away the wrap to fully reveal the object, I see that it's a beautiful silver statue of Pegasus, the winged horse of Greek mythology. Goose bumps cover my arms as I hold the figure in my hands. Choked, I place my hand over my mouth to stop myself from breaking down. Relieved to be alone, I look through teary eyes at the mythical steed, feeling overwhelmed. This ancient equine was on the insignia of 5 Airborne Brigade. Steeped in history, the paratroopers of that era stitched the old maroon-backed insignia into the inside of the collar on their smocks.

It's unheard of for a non-parachute-trained combat medic to receive the Pegasus; the significance of the gesture goes beyond any student of merit, distinction, or promotional board. No one ever tells you about the impact that you have on a situation – unless it's bad of course, like the black day sack. I never expected the airborne brethren to go so far outside of their historical traditions to ensure that I knew my place within their brigade. In short, it blows me away. Beaming, I continue packing. Leaving the statue to one side, I glance its way every couple of minutes.

Carving out a successful career in what is traditionally a man's world is never going to be easy, and like many before me, I am a proactive woman proving my worth through action and not words. Ever moving forward, I stopped asking for permission a long time ago.

Dusting off my suit, I prepare for my final day of military service. All is in order, right down to my pressed white shirt. Nevertheless, I am apprehensive about saying goodbye.

My last day of military service arrives: 30 June 2009. It is also the day that my good friend Sgt Phil Train is to be buried.

A small group of us gather at Yates Wine Bar on North Hill in Colchester's historic city centre. 'To Phil!' Glasses chink together, and shouts of 'cheers' sound across the bar.

The carpet beneath my feet is sticky. It's early morning, ordinarily not the time to be drinking Jack Daniels and Coke, but today is different, and the two double shots go down easy. The wine bar is close to St Peter's, the garrison church where the funeral will take place. Besides, this bar is the only place that's serving this early. A barmaid looks at our group inquisitively, disappearing through the staff-only door as we become loud. I take a chance to quickly dash upstairs to the toilet, through fear of getting caught short in a half hour or so. On my return, my hand is met by yet another shot of Jack and Coke.

'Ready?' Dave Eatock taps my shoulder. As recruit instructors the three of us were firm friends. Origionally 1 (PARA) Dave deployed to Helmand with 2 (PARA).

We make our way out onto the main street. Feeling a little light-headed, I reach for the spearmints in my bag. We walk the short distance down the hill towards St Peter's, stopping short to say hello to friends who are gathering outside. Walking through the huge wooden doors, I am handed a program listing the sequence of events. The church feels cold despite the bright sunshine outside; the building dates back to 1086.

Taking my seat, I see the familiar faces of friends sitting in the pews to my left. A flash of guilt comes over me for not having kept in touch. Paratroopers start to fill the rows in front, each holding his headdress in his hands. The deep maroon colour of their berets stands out against the backdrop of the dark wood shelving that houses the hymn sheets. A quiet hum of conversation fills the church as the soldiers chat quietly to one another. Several officers arrive, wearing their formal service dress, and ushers show them to their seats at the front of the church, close to Phil's family. The brigade commander arrives and takes his place alongside the other officers of 16 Air Assault Brigade HQ.

I start to feel the effects of the Jack Daniels and Coke, so it seems that my trip to the toilet is not all that I hoped it would be. For a moment, I drift off, wondering what today means. I feel angry that this is the way it will end for my good friend Phil Train. Phil was a paratrooper who served with 2nd Battalion, the Parachute Regiment (2 PARA). Like me, he was born in Plymouth, where his mother, Phyllis, and his brothers, Jason and David, still live. A quiet man with silver-grey hair and piercing blue eyes, Phil was determined, confident, and at ease with himself.

When we met, I immediately sensed an air of something

different about him, something special. Firstly, his kit and equipment always looked better than others', and he didn't have an endless stream of pouches on his belt kit. The words 'if I don't need it, I don't carry it' are never far from my thoughts when I think of him. Phil was attached to the army training depot in Bassingbourn. We had both been selected for a tour of duty as recruit instructors.

The very best in our training company, he gave me what I had so often longed for in the past: someone to learn from. In the early days of my army service, I always lacked female role models, which left me to learn my craft from the blokes. It always appeared to me that most women serving back then didn't know how to pitch. They either tried too hard and became overbearingly butch, or, through lack of character, they didn't try hard enough. I soon learnt, though, that a fair few of the guys lacked character as well. Soldiering should come naturally. You can train a skill all day long; what you can't train is an attitude.

Learning from Phil saved my life. Many of my friends ask what it's like to be a woman in the military. I believe it's all about balance, but sometimes it's easy to get the balance wrong. It took me a long time to realise that. I have been on every level: too much, too little, and, finally, just right. I credit most of my achievements with being brought up properly, albeit in a less-fortunate area. This gave me the drive and determination to succeed. But it was Phil who taught me by example how to finesse my strengths into the balance I needed.

I copied Phil, and soon I was amazed at how much easier life became when I learnt how to soldier from a soldier. My manner became more assertive, and I started to look at things differently. Medicine is my forte and the area that I am expert in, but other aspects of soldiering are equally important. I had to learn how to employ good medicine in a tactically unstable environment.

Phil helped immeasurably. His leadership was crucial to the young paratroopers deployed with him in Helmand during our summer tour of 2008. The 2 PARA suffered heavy losses when fighting increased during the fighting season. The two of us spent many hours exchanging war stories when we passed through Camp Bastion on our way home, chatting at length outside the little coffee shop. I've already described this briefly; now, sitting at his funeral, the moments we shared replay in my mind.

The worst thing about today is getting my head around Phil's senseless death. He survived the notorious Sangin Valley, only to be killed in a motorbike crash at home. In my eyes, a man like Phil should die as a grandfather telling war stories, unless he was KIA. If this warrior had to die young, it should have been on the battlefield.

The sound of the church organ interrupts my private thoughts, its sombre notes drawing my eyes to the left. I see six paratroopers marching slowly, bearing Phil's coffin to the front of the church. My support weapons teacher noted earlier, Paul Scott ('Scotty'), is among the pallbearers, along with Cpl Matty Desmond. The pain of losing Phil is etched on their faces. All of us are interlinked somewhere along the line. As they make their way forward, all heads turn to look at the coffin. If their thoughts are anything like mine, images of Phil must be flashing through their minds.

Phil's young wife, Stacy, stands silently, her head held high. Her dignified manner is a credit to the husband that she is saying goodbye to. Phil's coffin is lowered onto its support. One by one, people stand to speak about Phil, each describing his honour and bravery. Then someone reads a simple statement. I don't recall now who spoke the words, but I remember smiling at the truth of them: 'He was a good bloke.' This meant more than a medal or an overthought speech. That was it. Phil was a good bloke, and that's how he should be remembered.

The service then moves on to Colchester Cemetery, a short drive away. The traffic is busy, and local people stand and watch the funeral cortege taking Phil's coffin through the streets. In addition to being the oldest recorded town in England, Colchester is a garrison town. The small population is extremely supportive of 'their paratroopers', as they fondly regard the blokes.

As we drive through the gates of the cemetery, the sky is bright and the grounds are peaceful. We make our way into the crematorium, and Phil's men once again carry his coffin, bringing it into the small room. Suddenly and without warning, a song starts to play. The words to Mariah Carey's 'Hero' are louder than I would have expected, and the lump in my throat comes loose. I struggle to hold it together, and all the pomp and ceremony offer no comfort. Outside, soldiers from 2 PARA fire a salute to Phil, and the volley is deafening. Trying hard to compose myself, I fumble in my bag, realising that I don't have any tissues. What an idiot! I stand there, wiping my face on my jacket sleeve like a four-year-old. Throughout all of my time serving, I always prided myself on keeping it together.

As the tears stream down my face, I let myself feel the grief that I usually suppress during such moments. I am a combat medic accustomed to dealing with blood and death and the 'less glamorous' side of life. That is far different from facing the death of a loved one or a dear friend.

Phil's not a picture on the news; his death is not an 'event', so to speak. Looking at his lovely wife, I wonder how she will cope, how she will even begin to rebuild a life without him. As soldiers, we come to expect that the worst might and could happen, but I don't believe that we truly understand the void that we leave behind. Stacy is one of many young wives having to rebuild their lives alone. The same is true for many first-time mothers, long-time spouses, and grieving parents – the list of loved ones left behind is endless.

I never really thanked Phil for all that he had done for me. Seeing him a few days prior to the accident, we joked about his hosting the next barbecue. Never in a million years did I think that I would never see him again. If I had, I surely would have at least said 'thank you' – and those simple words would have meant so much more. Knowing Phil, he realised that. I will always put much of what I have achieved as a soldier down to the time I spent learning from him when we were posted as instructors. Carrying that forward is the way that I will honour my friend and mentor.

Our group heads back to 2 PARA sergeants' mess, where Phil's friends and family have gathered. A huge screen flashes photos of Phil, and soon the drinks start to flow. I see many familiar faces, having been based at Merville Barracks in Colchester, Essex, for the last three years. Colchester is home to many units which form the brigade.

Having made lifelong friends among all units, I know that I will always be welcome here. The combination of the funeral and the end of my military service puts me in a reflective state of mind. I start thinking about my days of service, especially my time in Afghanistan.

In Helmand, I became frustrated by the lack of resources and manpower which left us exposed in 2006. Things did not improve much over time. In 2008, our lack of helicopters forced us to drive around in lightly armoured vehicles, travelling on roads that the Taliban had littered with their crude, destructive roadside bombs. Our government had an almost naive military appreciation that we, task force Helmand, controlled the battle space. In reality, the insurgents had the tactical advantage, and every boot on the ground knew that.

Back in 2006, I recall then Defence Secretary John Reid saying that he hoped not a single round would be fired on that tour. Clearly, he had been reading the wrong reports: it was hugely kinetic, and firefights with insurgents were a daily occurrence.

The first brigade into Helmand, led by Brig. Ed Butler, faced significant challenges. By the end of the tour, it was clear that the brigade's main fighting force, 3 PARA battle group, had delivered a significant measure of tactical success. 3 PARA achieved this under the command of Lt Col Stuart Tootal, although with very few resources, our brigade suffered heavy casualties. The insurgents identified that they could not fight and win in face-to-face running battles with the West, so by the end of the summer of 2006, attacks on UK forces were significantly reduced.

Intelligence indicated that the enemy had taken a severe beating, seriously depleting their manpower. Coupled with the change in seasons, this indicated that the insurgency might need a new strategy to disrupt and yet not necessarily overcome the strength of Western forces.

In a statement, Brig. Butler's spokesman at the time told the media: 'There is evidence that the Taliban's tactical capability to mount large attacks on the battlefield has been seriously degraded. But they remain a significant threat and the use of improvised explosive devices is a major concern.'

A forewarning for what was yet to come was not acknowledged by the white collar decision makers in Whitehall, and by late 2006, the Taliban had changed their tactics, with more attention given to the roadside bomb. They opted for smaller operations in which they planted countless IEDs, and the volume of attacks on coalition forces soared.

When 3 Commando Brigade took over the reins of Helmand Province in October 2006, many soldiers and senior officers hoped that the political aim would be to support the military with additional force. In military jargon, this is known as 'reinforcing success' – in simple terms, it means putting more resources into the battle to deny the enemy the chance to regroup or reorganise any form of resurgence. Despite requests from Brig. Butler to deploy more troops and resources, none arrived.

The failure to quickly reinforce the brigade's success by deploying more helicopters, more troops, and better equipment led to an insurgency stronger than anyone would ever care to admit. The UK government failed its fighting troops and only marginally increased the level of men on the ground. We sent nearly 40,000 into Iraq in 2003 yet could only muster 3,500 for Afghanistan in 2006; this number eventually rose to 10,000, a far cry from the figure that was actually required.

In 2010, four years after my first tour, the Americans deployed more than 25,000 troops to Helmand, lifting the coalition manpower level to more than 35,000, with the UK contribution at around 10,000. History may later suggest that this was the number that was needed when we first entered southern Afghanistan.

Road moves were our biggest danger, especially as there was no national curfew imposed. This easily employed tactic would have removed the cover of night given to insurgents to plant bombs. The lack of additional air assets gave us little chance of reinforcing any success. Helicopters provide commanders with speed and surprise. They are essential in dominating an enemy, especially in areas of difficult terrain, such as southern Afghanistan.

Our initial choice of armoured vehicles provided limited protection against IEDs and RPGs. Our mechanics added metal plates which gave more protection; unfortunately, the weight reduced their capability and speed. It also put huge strain on gearboxes. Even with the best armour, travelling across open desert created unique problems. The tracks of our vehicles cut a path through the sand, creating a huge sand cloud that signalled to everyone, Taliban included, that we were in the area. No surprise and no speed.

The Soviets suffered catastrophic losses during their invasion of Afghanistan in 1979. They poured armoured vehicles into the country, but the tactic failed. Many of their tanks still sit all across the country, stark reminders of the disastrous incursion. The mujahideen, the enemy at that time, placed mines and roadside bombs too, mounting attack after attack on Soviet vehicles, killing thousands of their soldiers.

Beginning in 2007 and into 2008, the UK adopted the same policy of using large numbers of armoured vehicles, and the number of deaths from IEDs soared. Had we not already learnt these lessons? The fighting man on the ground was let down by politicians who failed to understand the problems the military faced and failed to respond quickly to requests for more troops and equipment. Our commanders were not afforded the faith that they so urgently needed.

For me as a medic, the resources – or, rather, the lack of them – at the makeshift hospital in Camp Bastion during the summer of 2006 provided perfect examples of this. We had limited capability for dealing with serious wounds, particularly head injuries, which forced us to fly men to Kandahar to be treated by the Canadians. The sole reason that the brigade fared so well medically has much to do with the willingness and foresight of all hospital staff and support to adapt and overcome any shortfalls. Young medical officers and surgeons pioneered treatments, saving the lives of soldiers who ordinarily would have been lost. But it wasn't just lack of general equipment and medical resources that inhibited care, it was inadequate rescue capability too.

Our lack of rescue capability was further highlighted when a patrol became trapped in an unmarked legacy minefield. (A legacy minefield is one which has been left behind by previous conflicts.) After a catalogue of disastrous events, four severely injured men, including my good friend Stu Pearson, had to lie in a minefield for an unacceptable length of time. This should not have been allowed to happen.

I recall returning to Kandahar from my mid-tour leave at the time of the incident. It was early in the morning when I heard the news about Stu. I was desperate to get back to the hospital at Camp Bastion so I could see him and make sure that he was okay. The following day, I booked in at the airhead and boarded an RAF Hercules for the short forty-minute journey to Camp Bastion. As the flight touched down on the airstrip, I couldn't wait to get off. Hurrying from the transport, I quickly dropped my kit off in the tented accommodation close to the hospital. Heading straight for the high-dependency unit, I asked one of the nurses where I could find Stu.

Nothing prepared me for the sight of him lying there. Walking through the canvas doors of the ward in Camp Bastion was one of the most emotionally charged moments of my life. Feeling unsteady on my feet, I couldn't control myself. I looked at Stu and mumbled, 'You alright?' Unable to keep it together, I started to cry as Stu looked up at me. There are moments in life when you need to be strong and resolute, and there are other moments when you just need to let it go. I think the tears came through sheer relief; I was just so relieved that Stu was still alive.

His eyes were glazed and watery because he was high on medication, but he knew that he was in a bad way. With one leg already amputated, there was a strong possibility that he would lose the other one. Lying in the next bed was Cpl Stu Hale, also missing a leg; next to him was another amputee, Fus. Andy Barlow. The four others injured that day were on the general ward on the other side of the tented hospital corridor. Another good friend and a fellow medic, Cpl Paul ('Tug') Hartley, was also wounded. Luckily, Tug had avoided loss of limb.

I left the room to compose myself. Wiping my face, I took a few deep breaths and went back in, only to find myself struggling to find the right words. In the end, I just waffled on about my leave and other nonsense. What are you supposed to say in these circumstances? I wanted to give Stu a hug, let him know that everything was going to be okay. But he was covered from head to toe in tubes and dressings, so I just held his hand. I didn't like that he was the only one still awake; the others all looked so peaceful, and yet Stu had to sit and contemplate all that had happened.

He kept asking me about his other leg, concerned that he was going to lose it. This gave me a much-needed purpose: I set about getting answers from surgeons about his chances. The initial response wasn't great. They were doing all that they could to save the second limb, but the damage was severe. I was advised that the chances of saving the second leg were fifty-fifty; most of it would be down to the healing post-surgery, and infection control was a huge factor.

Before his evacuation, I stayed with Stu. I had to be sure that he didn't die. Sometimes people roll through life blinkered that the worst will never happen to them – but it can and it does.

Sitting by Stu, I was angry that we weren't better equipped to deal with this type of incident. When we send our heaviest helicopter to a minefield, troops on the ground see it, momentarily feeling relieved that they are going home. But then the bird flies off again because its downdraught may set off other mines.

This was often exactly what happened. And that's how it was for Stu and the others. A mine was set off, killing Cpl Mark Wright. Lying trapped in that minefield, Mark died from his injuries. With no combat search and rescue (CSAR) helicopter to winch the injured soldiers to safety, our commanders were left with no choice but to do what soldiers always do: get on with the job and deal with the incident by using the equipment that was available. The Americans saved the day again, deploying two Black Hawks to carry out the rescue of our stricken soldiers. The aircraft flew to the scene from Kandahar, some forty minutes away.

Our system, or lack of one, had failed. The incident left Cpl Stu Pearson (3 PARA), LCpl Stu Hale (3 PARA), and Fus. Andy Barlow (Royal Regiment of Fusiliers [RRF]) with lower limb amputations. Cpl Mark Wright was posthumously awarded the George Cross (GC) for his outstanding bravery and leadership during the incident. Stu Pearson was decorated with the Queen's Gallantry Medal (QGM). Andy Barlow and Paul Hartley were both awarded the George Medal (GM). All members of the patrol told of how Mark wouldn't let them fall asleep during their four-hour wait for rescue. This alone had much to do with the fact that any of them survived at all.

Significantly, the patrol never would have gone near the minefield that day had they been given an up-to-date map of the area. This data was available but not provided. As I walked then Commanding Officer Lt Col Stuart Tootal down the long, dark corridor of the tented hospital to formerly identify Mark,

I felt awkward. Offering a cup of tea seemed appropriate. He accepted politely as most senior officers would. Identifying all of his fallen with humility and respect, his was an unenviable task.

Although I continued to serve through 2009, the experience of Stu and the others left me doubtful that I could endure much more of the bullshit coming out of the mouths of politicians who were involved in decision making at the top. When brigadiers and commanding officers destined for great things start resigning, that tells me that things aren't as they should be.

I never thought that I would muster the courage to move on, but my intuition told me that it was time to go. The army helped shape me, and having experienced so much during the eleven years that I served, I wondered if any other career could satisfy me, mentally or physically.

Following Phil's funeral on my last day of military service, I set about formulating my plans for the future. The world of private security appeals to me the most; it seems the perfect bridge between leaving the forces and becoming a civilian again. I use as much of my resettlement time as possible to qualify in areas that are less familiar to me. Luckily, my trade as a combat medic is in great demand. I undertake training to become a close protection operative, soon securing employment with an American company operating out of Afghanistan. Thus, in September 2009, just a year after returning home, I find myself preparing to make my way back to Afghanistan, the country that has flooded the UK and Europe with its biggest export: heroin.

Using my final weeks wisely, I spend as much time with loved ones as possible. Losing Phil, someone so close, has again reminded me never to take friends or family for granted. I know that seeing them again before Christmas is highly unlikely.

The day of my departure arrives quickly, and once again, I

leave my familiar world. At London's Heathrow, I say goodbye to my fiancé at the security gate, knowing that this is the beginning of the end for us. Ryan wants a simple life, and I want to escape the normality that I so obviously struggle to deal with. Like most couples, we pressed on whilst our relationship was in trouble, perhaps for a year or so. But my decision to return to Afghanistan has ended any hope of saving what we had. Although extremely hard, it would turn out to be the best decision for both of us.

Afghanistan, a country written off by the rest of the world, is a place where I feel comfortable. Eventually, being there will help me heal the psychological wounds that I have continually blocked out.

Making a short stopover in the United Arab Emirates, I am overwhelmed by the magnitude of the city of Dubai. Their impressive infrastructure momentarily disguises a world of over indulgence and double standards.

My transfer to Kabul is swift, and before I know it, we touch down at Kabul International Airport (KAIA). As the hydraulic doors lift, the familiar smell of diesel and death hit me like a freight train.

It feels different being here without the instant respect that my British army uniform gave me; gone, too, was the rank that I had earned in that uniform. The ANP providing security at the airport view me with suspicion, and it is a look that I do not appreciate.

I'm travelling with two other medics, both former military. Taff is former Royal Navy, and Robbie served as a combat medic with the Australian army. As we get in line to collect our baggage, they are as apprehensive as I am.

I created this situation for myself. Conscious that I don't have a weapon, my palms are sweaty. Getting eyes on the personal security detail moving us to our new home further highlights what is now my inner turmoil. The ground brief and actions on contact and casualties I receive from a dangerously overweight personal security detail (PSD) lead is a world away from the start I envisioned. To make matters worse, I acknowledge that I have no medical kit. Desperate to call my regiment, I wonder what they would think if they knew that I was out here cutting about with no weapon to protect myself.

We set off driving through the dusty roads of Kabul, and all the signs of the destruction left behind after numerous roadside bombs scar the landscape and the faces of the local populace. It has always amazed me how the Afghan people continue to go about their daily business.

Scanning around and looking for any dangers, I check windows for gunmen, alleyways for potential threats, motorcycles getting too close. It's then that I realise that Kabul is very different from the Afghanistan that I am familiar with. Thinking about the last time that I moved by road here, I feel suddenly overwhelmed by regret, wondering if my decision to return will somehow bite me in the arse. Taking a deep breath, I get a grip of myself. Yes, I am no longer military, but that is no excuse to start acting like a sack of shit.

I come up with a workable plan, identifying that there are plenty of weapons in the vehicle. In the event of the worst, I would probably get the overweight commander's M4 American assault rifle, as there is no way on earth that he could get out of the vehicle quickly enough to be effective. It's still early September, and the heat of Kabul is not as uncomfortable as the heat of Helmand Province was in late July 2008. Laughing to myself about my mini panic attack just moments before, I calm down, reminded of Nad-e Ali and B Company.

On arrival at our new home, we are met by our senior

medical officer, Tom, a former US special ops medic (or 18D), a man I would come to respect very much. Posted to an outstation in the east of the country, Jalalabad would remain my home for the following eighteen months. I received a medical curriculum from which I devised a workable training plan. After teaching three junior doctors who would assist me, the four of us trained the Afghan border police combat medics.

My medics were being pushed out to fight on the eastern front, high up in the hills that border Pakistan. It was a huge undertaking for us all: translations had to be accurate and swift, and we only had a short time allocated for each medical cadre.

Some might say that I am addicted to the path of most resistance. Initially not taken seriously on account of my sex, I set about getting as physically fit and strong as possible. I went back to Kabul to complete the Department of State (DOS) protective security detail course before returning to Jalalabad.

On my first day back, a naval corpsman called Fig meets me. He will take on the role as my 2IC when teaching the Afghans. Fig is attached to the US Marines assigned to our FOB. Together, we instil physical and mental discipline into all of our students. We run them ragged around our compound daily, in searing heat and full fighting order, ensuring that they understand the importance of the medical packs that they carry on their backs.

'Hey, Channy, where are you taking them today?' Fig laughs as he negotiates the six-foot wall, with all of his kit on his back.

When he is done with our guys, I put my medical pack on my back, indicating to the Afghans that they should follow me. I do this by using a genuine smile and hand signals. Afghans are hard, resilient people who live rough for all of their relatively short lives. They respond positively when effectively guided.

Responsible for the medical care of our isolated FOB, I soon become the lead trauma medic for a site of up to a thousand personnel (when fully manned). Jalalabad is a beautiful place, and a healing one for me. Going back to basics has been restorative, and I've started to heal the mental scarring that I never even realised existed.

In addition, I am giving something back to the Afghans. I am not housed in their school or using their well water, but I have learnt to enjoy their culture. Working alongside the Americans is an experience that I will later recall fondly. Surrounded by generous, forgiving, and, above all, loyal people, there is always fun to be had. During the Fourth of July celebrations, my suggestion of running around the FOB in a redcoat has everyone roaring with laughter. Spending many hours watching Kenny Powers with my Marine Corps muckers allows me to hold on to my military past for a bit longer.

Every Afghan I have taught will shake my hand firmly before leaving our FOB. I have found this humbling. I understand all too well that they head to places that many of them would never return from. They respect that I was in Helmand, often asking me what it was like. I will never understand how they truly saw me, but they did become my brothers by choice, and I know that they will never forget me.

I have chosen this life less ordinary. It may not be politically correct, and at times I wish that I had selected something a little easier. I demand a great deal from myself, and it will take a lot to fulfill my dreams and shape my destiny. Always learning, never waning, I am a proactive woman. I will continue to break down barriers so that future generations have the right to choose.

Once again, I prepare to leave Afghanistan, this time to embark on the very different avenue of diplomatic protection. As I depart, I heed the advice that up until now has always served me best: I will never become a product of my environment; my environment will always be a product of me.

ABOUT THE AUTHOR

Chantelle specialises in the provision and effective implementation of medicine in unstable or hostile regions, she is an ambassador for GBV UNCOVERED an international online think tank dedicated to improving the medical and psychological care available to the survivors of sexual gender-based violence [GBV] in the world's conflict regions. Using the best principles of remote and hostile medicine, emerging technologies and innovations their goal is to develop robust, cheap and easily reproducible solutions including physical and psychological first aid protocols and portable medical kit for use by grass-roots NGOs assisting female survivors within the golden 72 hours post-assault.

The former Combat Medic had a remarkable career in the British Army. Renowned for being the first British female soldier in history to engage and kill an enemy combatant at close quarters, she was the lead medic supporting an infantry fighting company during prolonged combat operations in the notorious region of Helmand Province, Afghanistan.

Chantelle's passion to support and empower women comes from a credible background operationally covering the Balkans, Africa, Asia and the Middle East. On leaving the service she was recommended to take the Queen's commission from the ranks before returning to Afghanistan for a third time with the U.S. Department of State, Chantelle developed from inception the trauma assistant program completing two years as an instructor in combat medicine. Moving to Baghdad, Taylor transitioned into diplomatic security and for a further four years she undertook the role of primary protection officer for the Australian Ambassador to Iraq. Chantelle is looking forward to undertaking a Masters next year in Security, Terrorism and Intelligence at Kings College in London.

Battleworn along with the author's poem 'Keep me Awake' was featured as part of the British militaries contribution on display at the Warrior Care exhibition held in Washington DC.

In Arduis Fidelis

Manufactured by Amazon.ca
Bolton, ON